We Love You Liverpool We Do

We Love You Liverpool We Do

Edited by David Lane

Meyer & Meyer Sport

British Library Cataloguing in Publication Data
A catalogue record for this book is available from the British Library

We Love You Liverpool We Do
Maidenhead: Meyer & Meyer Sport (UK) Ltd., 2014
ISBN 978-1-78255-037-2

© 2014 by Meyer & Meyer Sport (UK) Ltd.
Aachen, Auckland, Beirut, Budapest, Cairo, Cape Town,
Dubai, Hägendorf, Indianapolis, Singapore, Sydney, Tehran, Wien
Member of the World Sport Publishers' Association (WSPA) www.w-s-p-a.org
Printed by: B.O.S.S Druck und Medien GmbH, Germany
ISBN 978-1-78255-037-2
E-Mail: info@m-m-sports.com
www.m-m-sports.com

Contents

Introduction

In 1978, I joined Liverpool Football Club and spent seven years playing over 350 league and cup games. I scored in two European Cup finals and in other finals, too. I loved every minute of my time at the club and wish I was still playing for them now. It was an honour and a privilege to play for a club that was so well run off the pitch and who were European Champions on the pitch. I knew from my England colleagues Terry McDermott, David Fairclough and Phil Thompson how special Liverpool Football Club was before I joined them, but not until I started playing for Liverpool did I realise that the standard of football was second to none. As a player, I was always proud to pull on the red shirt and give 100 percent in every game. The fans were always behind you if you did this, even if the football you played was not as good as you would have liked. Liverpool fans always show their appreciation to players who try their best for the club. The fans could win you the game sometimes, and I was fortunate to play regularly at Anfield in front of crowds over 50,000 with over 25,000 fans urging me on from the famous Kop. I still work for the club now, and I understand the importance of it in people's lives be they local, from Norway, Ireland or just about anywhere in the world. I work with other former players, such as John Barnes and Phil Neal, promoting the club to the next generation of fans. I had a great, great time at Liverpool FC as a player, and I want people to know what a great club it is. I would like to thank Liverpool Football Club for my memorable playing career and for the support it now gives me and other former players to promote the club to the fans of the future. Please enjoy the book.

Alan Kennedy

OUR FATE & DESTINY

My wife Gayner and I have been loyal Liverpool supporters for more than 35 years. In fact, I have been following the Reds since 1969 and am probably one of the few who has attended five European Cup finals, although I did not go to Heysel. Gayner and I met following tragic circumstances at Valley Parade, the home of Bradford City, in May 1985. We were both in the main stand that caught fire and, tragically, claimed many lives. Gayner was in the middle of a stampede, amidst the great heat and confusion, with hundreds of people fleeing for their lives. She could not get over the wall and onto the pitch to safety as the fire raged across the wooden stand. As the flames were getting closer, policemen appeared to help people to safety with their uniforms and, in one case, hair on fire. The stampede intensified as families became separated and Gayner lost sight of her father. The smoke from the inferno obscured the vision of supporters who had now begun to realise that the exit gates at the back of the stand were locked and that there was no way out. All of a sudden, a tall man with dark shoulder-length hair wearing a blue leather jacket appeared and lifted Gayner over the wall and away from the biting flames. Thankfully Gayner's father also survived the flames, and they were reunited on the pitch. Gayner and I met a few months later at a function where, as she describes it, she recognised the dark-haired man with the blue leather jacket who saved her life. We've been married for more than 20 years now and are practically inseparable. This was obviously kismet, our fate and destiny, as we quickly discovered that we were both big Liverpool fans and were at Valley Parade with friends for Bradford City's game with Lincoln City on the final day of the season. The tragedy of Valley Parade was one of the low points of my life, but Gayner and I were among the lucky ones—56 lives were lost on that dreadful day in May 1985, and it is a tragedy that still haunts me as much as the Hillsborough disaster, which of course is profound for all Liverpool supporters all over the world. Our story has never been published, and I never in my wildest dreams thought I would meet my future wife at a football match—never mind during one of football's biggest disasters.

LEARNING THE RULES OF THE KOP

I was just seven years old when my father first took me to Anfield. It was 2 February 1957, and Liverpool were playing Middlesbrough in the old Second Division. It was good of my dad to take me, as he was an Evertonian. I know what I would have told my son had he asked to be taken to Goodison Park—fortunately he never did! We watched the match from the rickety old Kemlyn Road Stand, which was replaced in 1963. The crowd that day was 38,890, not bad for the Second Division. Liverpool lost 2-1, and I was less than impressed with the team, apart from goalkeeper Tommy Younger and left-half Geoff Twentyman, who, head wrapped in bloodied bandages, performed heroics in defence. His injury was caused by an early clash of heads with Brian Clough. Clough, however, did not reappear after the pair were stretchered off. There were no substitutes in those days, but Liverpool still lost to the 10 men of Borough.

The team might not have been great, but I was totally awestruck by the Kop, not just by the size of the terracing, but by the noise that emanated from it whenever Liverpool attacked that end of the ground. I dreamed of standing on the Kop, soaking up the atmosphere, but the Kop was no place for a seven-year-old, or indeed for any youngster below teenage years.

Over the next few years, I gradually became a regular, standing on the Kemlyn Road terraces or at the Anfield Road end. When I was feeling flush, I would stand in the Paddock below the Main Stand, and, when I was short of cash, I would pluck up courage and visit the Boys' Pen situated in the corner where the Kop joined the Main Stand. The Boys' Pen had a bit of a reputation, and I always ensured that I had sufficient change for the bus home hidden in my socks in case I should fall foul of one of the disreputable characters who inhabited the Pen. Fortunately, I never needed to call on the 'sock fund'!

After many near misses, Liverpool eventually achieved promotion to the old First Division in the 1961-62 season, a feat which caused wild rejoicing on the red side of Merseyside. We would now have the opportunity to play against elite teams such as Tottenham Hotspur, Everton, Manchester United and Burnley—yes, Burnley were a top team in those days, having won the League in 1960, and it was the abolition of the maximum wage that was to relegate the small town clubs to 'also rans'. And Liverpool had drawn Burnley in the fourth round of the 1962/63 FA Cup. The Reds had struggled to find their feet at the higher level initially, but, by New Year, they were comfortably placed in mid-table, and the FA Cup promised an exciting diversion from the league battles. The first leg at Turf Moor was played on 26 January 1963, and ended in a 1-1 draw. So it was back to Anfield for a midweek replay, a match that was delayed until 20 February by the big freeze of that infamous winter. Under-soil heating was still a thing of the future.

It seemed that everyone wanted to attend this particular match, and there would be no time for me to go home to have my tea after school or to do my homework. I would have to make my way straight to the ground from school in Prescot and would suffer the ignominy of wearing my school uniform to the match. Two of my classmates, Geoff Nulty and Kenny Poole, were also going to the match, so we teamed up together. Geoff was a brilliant footballer and was later to play at the highest level with Burnley, Newcastle and Everton, captaining both the Magpies and Toffees. However, at the age of 13, he was definitely a Red. Kenny was not a great footballer, but he was the best fast bowler in our year, with an action similar to Lancashire's Bryan Statham.

We arrived at the ground at about 5pm and made our way to the Anfield Road end where we found a lengthy queue. As we progressed towards the back of the line of people, we began to realise that our chances of getting through the gates at this end of the ground were negligible, so we decided to set off and see if the queues for other parts of the ground were any shorter. They were just as long elsewhere, but we reckoned that we had a better chance if we joined one of the queues for the Kop, as its capacity was double that of the Anfield Road end—if we were successful this would be my first visit to the famous Kop!

Liverpool Football Club was not used to hosting big matches at that stage, and the organisation that evening left a lot to be desired—in later years it would have been all ticket, but the club seemed to have underestimated the likely attendance, and you could pay at the gate. Nobody thought to open the gates early, and there was a danger the ground would still be filling up beyond the kick-off time of 7.30pm—the queue moved very slowly, everybody desperate to get to the front and into the match. Ten minutes before the start, we finally passed through the turnstiles and began to climb the steps, but we heard loud shouting from behind us because the turnstiles had been closed—only a couple of dozen more fans had got through behind us. Almost 58,000 fans were inside the ground—a figure that has not been matched since that evening. We didn't get much farther, stopping close to one of the entrances near the top of the Kop, but it was blocked with fans. There seemed no way through. We heard the roar as the teams took to the pitch, and we heard an even bigger roar as the match kicked off, but we were still on the wrong side of the terraces. We had a wonderful view of the lights of the city if we looked over our shoulders, but no view of the action whatsoever!

It was at this point that a good old Liverpool docker came into his own—a group of them had come through the turnstiles behind us, and there was no way they were going to miss the match. So, with one almighty heave, they began pushing forward, and, thanks to their efforts, we were propelled through the gap and had a bird's eye view of the luscious green pitch and the action. Not that the view was perfect by any means—there were pillars supporting the roof that got in the way and everyone in front seemed so much taller than me—but at least the heat generated by 28,000 Kopites ensured that I soon thawed out after standing for nearly two and a half hours in the cold February evening waiting to get into the ground. Liverpool were attacking the Kop end in the first half but the first meaningful action I saw happened at the opposite end of the pitch. A long free kick from the left was glanced into the Liverpool net by Burnley's blond-haired England striker, Ray Pointer. The goal was greeted with silence on the Kop, and I can't remember seeing anything of Ian St John's equaliser on the stroke of half-time, my view was blocked, but the roar that greeted it left my ear drums ringing throughout the interval.

I was quickly learning the unwritten rules of the Kop. The main rule was to avoid being pinned against a crush barrier at all costs. The ideal place to stand was with your back to the barrier. Unfortunately, everyone else had also worked this out, and these were always the first spaces filled once the gates had opened. A surge occurred every time the ball went into one of the corners of the pitch at the Kop end, as spectators jostled forward to view the action. The trick was to make sure you muscled your way backwards the second that each surge ended. That way you could usually work your way back a step or two at a time until you had your back to the barrier, or at least you were well away from the barrier in front of you. This required immaculate timing and a

LIVERPOOL

Ian St. John
INSIDE LEFT

good sense of balance—Lionel Messi would have been very much at home performing this manoeuvre!

If my view of proceedings on the pitch was limited, my compensation lay in the fantastic atmosphere generated from the famous terracing as Liverpool pressed for a winner. 'You'll Never Walk Alone' was still a little in the future, but we had our St John chant, and we roared our heads off. Nevertheless, Burnley were proving a hard nut to crack, and the match went into extra time. There were no penalty shoot-outs in those days, and, as the 120th minute approached, a second replay was very much on the cards. Then, in the final seconds Liverpool were awarded a penalty at the Kop end. Even today I can see in my mind's eye Ronnie Moran running up to take the kick—that was all I saw, though the roar from the crowd told me the ball had hit the back of the Burnley net.

Another great roar sounded a minute later as the referee blew the final whistle. Somehow, I had been reunited with Geoff and Kenny in the last few minutes of the match, and we were well placed near the exit to make a dash to Utting Avenue to catch a football special back to Old Swan where we made our way to the stop for the number 10 Prescot bus. There were a couple of fans in front of us at the bus stop who were earnestly discussing a second replay, as they had obviously left the ground before the final whistle. We tried to convince them that Liverpool had won, but they would not believe us. They couldn't have been Kopites—nobody left the Kop that night until the final whistle!

I left my friends on the bus as I got off at Longview. I was tired, dirty and hungry. I still had a 10-minute walk home, and there was the small matter of my homework to complete before I went to bed, but regardless, I was on a high following my introduction to the Kop. My parents didn't need to ask me who had won the match—they could tell from the big grin on my face! Happy days.

Nick Norris

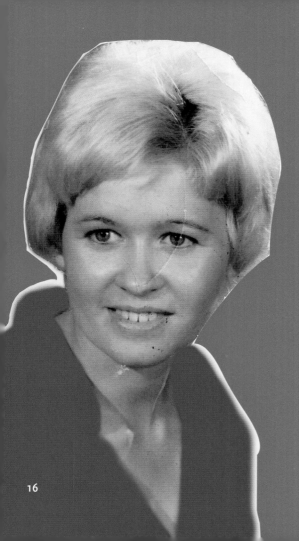

PARTY PEOPLE

Liverpool fans of a certain age will definitely remember, and will never forget, the wonderful 1977 European semi-final at Anfield when Liverpool beat Saint-Étienne. I lived in London at the time but was a staunch Liverpool fan. However, as I was born in Saint-Étienne, and my cousin and friends lived in the French city, they all decided to head over for the match, picking me up down south en route and continuing up to Merseyside.

However, as we approached Merseyside, we got hopelessly lost, and, by the time we eventually arrived at Anfield, we were rushing to get into the ground for kick-off. We frantically asked a policeman, who pointed us towards the Kop end, clearly not noticing the fact that my cousin had me dressed up in a Saint-Étienne jersey, scarf, hat and socks, along with the white hot pants I was wearing that day! As we entered the ground we thought it was best to make our way right to the front and stood behind the Saint-Étienne goal—thankfully nobody moaned about us being there.

The game was only five minutes in when Kevin Keegan made a run for Curkovic's goal and scored the most wonderful reverse-header I had ever seen. Seeing that I'd clapped and cheered the goal, the Liverpool fans right next to me asked me if I'd realised that my team had actually let one in, so I had to explain the rather confusing situation and the reason I had been made to wear my outfit. Anyhow, Keegan's was such a beautiful goal; it would have been incredibly biased not to have admired it somehow!

As the game progressed, many Liverpool fans in their colours came closer, and we all started to chat. And, after a while, I was asked to swap my scarf. I was happy to do so as my own Liverpool scarf was at home. Then another fan asked me to swap my hat; again, I was happy to oblige. Then another suggested that we swapped socks, so we did. And when Saint-Étienne scored their goal in the 3-1 defeat, one bold Liverpool supporter suggested we swapped jerseys, to which I replied: 'Sure, no problem' and just whipped mine off. However, those were the days when I didn't wear a bra! Not to worry, though, they were soon covered again, this time with a red top to match my face and that of the lad who'd asked me! I remember one fan took a photo of all his friends and me afterwards, a photo that I'd love to see all these years later.

When the match was over, lots of Reds fans congratulated us for the Bathenay goal, and, as we prepared to leave the ground, my family and friends were all invited to a party. In fact, that party led to an invite to another, then another, and we spent the next two days and nights in Liverpool being treated to the friendship and hospitality of the local people, which I'll never forget.

I've read so much rubbish that has been written about Liverpool fans over the years, but in my eyes, as one that has worn another team's jersey on the Kop, Liverpool is not only the greatest team in the world, they also have the best fans, too.

Roslyn O'Cionnaith *pictured left*

WE DID IT!
WE DID IT!

Wednesday 25 May 2005, it's 9am, and I'm in Istanbul. 'Fields of Anfield Road' has just gone off on my mobile phone, to wake me up, but I've been up since 6.30am—it feels like my wedding day. I check my phone, and there's a message from Tim sent at 5.45am: 'Just got to the airport. Don't worry. I've got your ticket.' Relief floods through me. I'm hungry, but I'm too nervous to eat, so I decide which shirt to wear: 2004/05 kit or T-shirt from Bangkok that reads 'Red Machine'. I go for the latter. I put on my grey Liverpool socks, which have become 'lucky' since the Juve and Chelsea games—I've never had lucky garments before. I even enjoy putting them on.

On the bus I meet Al. He is the largest Yorkshireman I have ever seen. 'Which part of Lancashire are you from?' I ask him in error. 'I'm not from tut Lancashire. Am from tut village near Huddersfield. Played tut rugby for tut Huddersfield tut when I was tut lighter. Now I'm tut 23 stone but lost two stone in tut two weeks.' I think Huddersfield sound like Rugby League but I have a feeling they're Rugby Union, but I decide not to ask him which. We arrive at the hotel and go to the rooftop restaurant for breakfast. It's not as nice as it sounds. Al tells me, 'I know we're tut going tut win. I don't know tut why. Just do!' He also says, 'Can't believe paid tut £1,200 for my tut flight!' Then he leaves, and I worry about Tim, who is travelling with my ticket.

It's now midday, and I'm thinking, 'Why hasn't Tim landed yet?' In truth, I can't remember when he's due in. I text him. Then I text James, then Maz, then Vikki. They are all on the European side of the city. I'm in Asia. At 12.30pm, I make my way west, over the Bosphorus, to Taksim Square where 30,000 Liverpool fans are waiting. I meet up with Maz and his mates, and they tell me not to worry, my ticket will arrive soon. I worry.

It's 2pm, and still no sign of Tim. I've sent him another message to tell him that I can't get onto the shuttle bus without a match ticket. I don't

really want to pay for a taxi, and I've heard that they're sending cabs with ticketless fans back to the city. Never mind the tension of a European Cup final, all I want is my tall, bespectacled Scouse mate to show up.

At 3.30pm I receive a message: 'Just landed, will send you a text when we're on the bus to Taksim. Tim.' I start breathing normally again. Twenty minutes later, I'm in a taxi on my way to the stadium. Tim's bus has been diverted directly to the ground, leaving me to haggle with a Turk whose name I don't ask. 'One hundred euro', he tells me. 'One hundred Turkish Lira?' I reply, pretending not to hear. 'NO! EURO!' he shouts back. I check my wallet, but I don't have one hundred euros. 'NO HAVE ENOUGH. ONE HUNDRED TURKISH?!' I'm desperate. He sees the desperation in my eyes and waves me in. He uses every single cab trick in the book to make the journey go faster and, somehow, I don't fear for my life.

Undertaking, overtaking on the wrong side of the road, skipping lights, cutting up everyone and anyone, beeping, beeping, beeping! On a dual carriageway, we pass an exit, he mutters 'Oh s****', breaks heavily and stops. He puts his hand behind my headrest and looks behind him. Surely not? He reverses back to the turning, causing traffic to swerve into the next lane. Part of me is in awe, part of me thinks of the driving test exam question: 'You miss your turning on the motorway. Do you A) Come off at the next exit? B) Reverse back up the hard shoulder, or, C) Do a U-turn in a gap in the central reservation?' At least he didn't do C.

It's 5pm as we approach the stadium, and policemen are waving us on. I wonder if all the taxis are being diverted away. Eventually, the ground comes into sight, and I question whether I should hide my red shirt with the $15 leather jacket I'd bought on my last trip to Istanbul. We approach a queue, and I can see dozens of policemen. They are checking every single car for tickets. ****! 'You hev ticket?' enquires my driver. I explain it's at the ground, and he seems to understand. We approach the police check. He doesn't stop, just drives right through them waving his arms as if he's carrying a VIP. They don't call him back—or shoot their guns. I breathe out. We are now about one kilometre from the ground, and fans are getting out of their cabs and are being checked for tickets again. I stay put. There is a cordon of officials asking each vehicle to wind down their windows. Mr Cabby of the Year pulls off the same trick.

The officials look confused, and, as we drive past them, I try to look confident and smile. My heart, which has almost stopped beating from lack of oxygen, resumes normal service. The taxi stops, and I open my wallet. I show him the contents of my wallet and tell him, 'This is all I've got.' I count out the notes. 'ONE HUNDRED EURO', he shouts at me. I give him another six million Lira (£2.40) and say, 'That's it! You have all my money now.' I leave the cab, dodge a big Turkish guy who'd poked his head through the window to see what the fuss was all about and don't look back.

As I enter a giant park reserved for the Liverpool fans, Tim sends me a message to let me know he's just arrived. I arrange to meet him at the PlayStation consoles. Twenty minutes pass, and I text him again. He's in the queue for programmes. I run to the stall, huge grin on my face. 'Jamie! Jamie!' I hear. I look up, and, in slow motion, I run to him and we embrace. I've never been so happy to see someone in my entire life. His friend, Andrew, has my ticket and hands it to me. I hold it for a few seconds, tightly, before putting it in my wallet. I hug Tim again and this time the hug is for him and for us and for being in Istanbul, at the final of the European Cup. There are still four hours to go until kick-off, and there are queues everywhere. Nobody is doing anything apart from queuing—there is a queue for the hot dogs, a queue for the programmes (which have run out because everyone has bought ten to flog on eBay), there's a queue for the portaloos, a queue for the PlayStation games and a queue for the official merchandising tent, which is turning into a scrum. The queues are crossing everywhere, and I'm not even sure people know what they're queuing for.

The road previously taking taxis to the stadium is now a winding red river—a torrent of Liverpool fans who are deserting their vehicles and marching, like an army, to the stadium. It is a rousing sight. Some fans, bored of queuing, have now climbed onto the tops of the portaloos. This is slightly less rousing. The area is filling and more and more people are talking about the game. I try not to listen. Thousands of people sing 'You'll Never Walk Alone', and I sway with the crowd. A man is climbing up a 30-ft pylon to attach a Union Jack to the top. I fear for his life. I also fear that if he does make it back down alive, he will be escorted out of the arena. On the other side of the park, fans are climbing onto the stage where the band is. An announcement: 'Will the Liverpool fans please make their way off the stage.' One minute later: 'The stage is full. Please leave the stage.' More fans pack onto the stage. 'This is a very dangerous situation. Please leave the stage. The stage will fall.' The fans start jumping on the stage. 'THE STAGE WILL COLLAPSE. PLEASE LEAVE THE STAGE!' More jumping. 'PLEASE LEAVE THE STAGE. THE STAGE WILL COLLAPSE AT ANY MOMENT!' The announcer changes tact and puts on a calm voice: 'If you do not leave the stage, it will collapse, and you will be hurt.' This does not appeal to the fans on the stage. There is a pause, and it sounds like the announcer is crying. Then, in what can only be described as an audition for the greatest monster movie of all time, the young Turk screams: 'LOOK OUT! THE STAGE IS COLLAPSING!' Liverpool fans stop jumping and look at the man with the microphone as if he is deranged. The stage is quite secure and not going anywhere. 'Ring of Fire' continues into the night...

With two and a half hours to go, the gates open. I'm a little apprehensive about being asked for my address by UEFA officials looking for tickets that have been passed on. As I am searched, my mind goes blank, and I can't even remember in which street in Liverpool Elliot lives, let alone his house number. Nobody asks me. At the gate, they are using the ticket bar code to activate the turnstile. Mine isn't working. The steward eventually gives up, tears my ticket and opens the gate manually. I'm in.

The sense of relief is overwhelming, and, for a moment, I completely forget why I'm actually here. I feel dehydrated and hungry, but the queue for food is ridiculous, so I walk down to my seat and take photographs. The stadium is breathtaking—a majestic superbowl arena fit for the final of finals. After half an hour, I go back up to the food stall and wait for about two minutes before giving up again. There are 100 people being served by five Turkish teenagers who don't speak much English, and everyone is pushing. So, to speed up their service, the chefs cut the burger cooking time from medium rare to pink with a hint of brown.

Forty-five minutes 'til kick-off, and I'm back in my seat, feeling a little faint. Three sides of the stadium have become a sea of red. It's going to be like a home game. I chat to the people either side of me, thinking, 'If I'm going to be kissing you at any point over the next couple of hours, at least let's get to know each other first', while simultaneously empathising with all the women I'd ever attempted to flirt with. A man approaches our seats, stares at his ticket and says, 'I think this is my seat.' The man next to me takes out his ticket. They have the same seat number but totally different looking tickets. One ticket clearly is not genuine. Right in front of a steward, they laugh, clasp hands, scream, 'YEHHHHHHS!' and resolve to stand in the aisle. 23

The opening ceremony reminds me of the significance of the match. Until now, the enormity of the game hasn't once punctured my psycho-safety bubble. I've thought about Gerrard lifting the cup, but when I have, I berate myself. The bubble is this—we are the underdogs; if we lose, it's because we've got Djimi Traore and not Paulo Maldini.

It's now near kick-off, and everything is happening too fast. 'You'll Never Walk Alone' is being sung out of sync so that I hear all three sides finish after the other, 'walk alohhhhne... walk alohhhhne... walk alohhhne...' I look over to the Milan fans, and they are as one. One voice, with flags handed out to form the three Milan colours. I glance over to the other half of my stand where someone has lit a red flare, and I hold my gaze as it fades. The roar of the crowd intensifies. When I turn, the game has already kicked off. I feel distracted and lost. After one minute, so do the players. The atmosphere has changed. Every single Liverpool fan expected to win, and now we have to contemplate not winning. Breaking down an Italian side, even with 90 minutes to go, seems like an impossible task. Some stop singing; arms fold. 'Ouch!' texts Howard, a barely part-time Manchester United fan from a farm in Hertfordshire.

The gulf in class is telling. Their patterns of play are becoming more and more elaborate, and they toy with us, much like a father playing football with his seven-year-old son, allowing us to attack knowing full well they could snatch the ball back at any moment, then twist and turn to tease and tease. Then the execution. And it is brutal. Not just 11 heads roll as Crespo strikes his second, but 50,000. We sink into our seats. Some battle cries go out, but we are sunk. Truly sunk. Then shame and embarrassment—we have proved ourselves to be the fifth best team in our league. I begin to think of my Milanese godfather, Tony, and his wife Maria. I'm quite proud to have an Italian godfather.

At half-time, a scuffle breaks out. A shirtless fan has run up and down the aisle, screaming: 'SING, SING, IT'S NOT OVER YET. SING. SINNNNG!' He approaches a scrawny looking guy who has his arms crossed and is looking as thoroughly depressed as everyone in the red half (or three-quarters, to be accurate) of the stadium. He yells in his face, 'COME ONNNNN!' The guy pushes him down the steps. He didn't want to do that to a man with more tattoos than sense. The tattoos came hurtling back up, stewards look on, laughing, and lots of people stand around saying sensible things like 'CHAAALM DOWN'. And lo, the words were spoken, and the ruffians did calmeth down. An anthem is a powerful thing, but it must be used sparingly, as if a secret weapon, if it is to be effective. Traditionally, 'You'll Never Walk Alone' is sung before every game. Sometimes, if the game is big enough, and the win is secured, it is sung in the final minutes. I can't remember hearing it during a game, but just before the end of half-time, we hear a corner of the ground singing, and we all rise, as one, with our scarves above our heads, and we sing. The sound of so many seats collapsing away was followed by one of the sweetest sounds mankind can produce—the rich, rich melody, the softness and yet the deep, deep resonance, and the unity among a 50,000-strong choir, pouring everything, absolutely everything, into a song. A song about hope. And now we are together.

Milan come out for the second half. The first of their players has his arms in the air, celebrating as if the game is over. If that were my player I would have liked him to be shot. The mood of the crowd has changed, and the players look to have been lifted. The Italians come close to their fourth. And then magic. A headed goal, a consolation, yet I react like that deranged Arsenal fan in the black leather jacket with the long curly hair. A primal outpouring of emotion. The second goes in. Who scored? What happened? Everything is becoming a blur. I put my head in my hands. I can't believe this. Penalty. Was it in the box? Is it a free-kick? NO! PENALTY! My hands are covering my mouth and nose. Now they are slowly making their way round the back of my head. They stay there, my elbows pointing to the play, then to the ground. Save! Goal! I am in a complete and utter state of joy. And we have 30 whole minutes to sing and blow the roof off this stadium—which to be honest, didn't have much of a roof to begin with. We're in football heaven, and we haven't even won the game. The remainder of the 90 flew by, and we're all still shaking our heads. I feel honoured to be present

at one of the greatest-ever European Cup finals, and if Milan are to score in extra time, there will be no shame now.

Milan step up the pace, and we look like a boxer on the ropes. Players go down with cramp, last-ditch tackles everywhere. In the very last minute of play, Dudek deflects the ball over the crossbar from two yards out. It is the most remarkable piece of action I think I have ever seen. I will never know how he did that. 'You'll Never Walk Alone' is sung for the sixth time. Dida walks towards the Milan end, and I recall that United lost in front of their own fans last week. 'We're about to watch the worst two nations at penalty shootouts...' I croak to my new friend next to me. I watch the worst penalty in the history of penalties sail over the bar. Oh my God.

A German steps up. The German does not miss. Ecstasy. Another Dudek save. Surely not. Cisse scores. Surely not. Milan score their first. Well, it wasn't going to be that easy. Riise misses... ****! Milan score. ****! ****! Smicer scores, again! Shevchenko places the ball down. I'm holding the person next to me very, very tightly. Shevchenko turns, he walks away from the ball and turns again to begin his run-up. I see the ball strike Dudek's leg. Has it rolled back into the goal? Everyone around me is jumping around. The players are running to their hero, the goalkeeper. We did it. We did it. Five!

Jamie Singer

THANK YOU FOR LAST NIGHT

This story is set in May 2005, just over a week before Liverpool's Champions League clash with AC Milan in Istanbul. At the time I was living and working on a British Army camp in Germany known as JHQ in Rheindahlen. Despite not being able to get to the game, I had been getting worked up and excited in the build-up to the final and was looking forward to flying the flag for Liverpool out in Germany.

During the day, I was approached by a sergeant who lived across the street from me, and he suggested that I should go home as he'd just seen my wife Amanda, who he said was visibly upset. So, worried and slightly confused, I headed off to see what was the matter. As I pulled up outside my house, Amanda was standing there waiting, and, as I got out the car, she came to the door to meet me. Her eyes were very red from crying, so I anxiously asked what was the matter. 'Mark, come in and sit down,' she said. Nothing could have prepared me for the news that my grandad had died that day, and at that point it felt as if my whole world fell apart. Amanda hugged me and tried to comfort me, but all I could think about was the last time I had seen him at our wedding, not even a month before. I went back to work as soon as I could to speak to my boss, Warrant Officer Hart, and told him what had happened. Without hesitation, he allowed me to take two weeks' compassionate leave, even though I knew I was not entitled to it. He said that I should be with my family, so we booked ourselves on the next overnight ferry from Rotterdam to Hull.

The European Cup final was played on the night before grandad's funeral, and, understandably, my head wasn't in the best of places. I have to admit that all the excitement I had felt previously as the game approached had virtually disappeared. In fact, I didn't feel like watching the game at all, but my immediate family felt that we couldn't just sit at home with so many mixed emotions, so we found ourselves at my parent's local, the Elm Tree pub. As we sat there in the bar area where my dad, grandad and I used to sit and have our Sunday afternoon drink together, I saw a small television in the corner, so I decided to turn the game on. I sat there watching the camera panning around the stadium, seeing the sea of red flags waving jubilantly—all hoping that Gerrard and company would lift the trophy again. But, as every Liverpool fan knows, it was not to be so easy. I collected a pint before moving to a table just in front of the TV to settle down to watch the game, trying to forget about what was coming in the morning. Then, as the game started, Amanda came over to join and support me. She had been brought up as a Manchester United fan by her dad, but, despite that, she sat next to me, held my hand and said, 'I've got a good feeling about this game.' When Maldini scored, I didn't feel too worried, as there were another 89 minutes to go, but as goals two and three went in, combined with the low of the past week, I was totally dejected. I got up, went to the bar and decided to drown my sorrows. I also decided to watch the second half from a stool at the bar, but Amanda, who is always my emotional rock, suggested we should go back to our original position in front of the TV. I said that there was not much point, to which she replied, 'Don't worry, Liverpool will score, I can feel it.' But, at that point, I thought that one goal was no more than a consolation and would be almost meaningless.

Then, 11 minutes into the second half, Amanda's prediction came true—Liverpool's rock, Steven Gerrard, heading in John Arne Riise's cross. I exhaled a sarcastic 'YEAH!' Again, as ever, Amanda tried to pick me up, 'Told you Liverpool would score!' I replied with a reality check, 'We still need two more goals just to even get a draw!' Amanda was having none of it. 'Don't worry, they will score again', and as her sentence finished, Smicer scored Liverpool's second. We looked at each other, I smiled, and, at that point, the impossible started to looked possible—could Liverpool really come back and win this thing? 'Penalty!!!!' I screamed as Steven Gerrard was brought down inside the area, and I started pacing backwards and forwards, willing Alonso to smash it into the back of the net. 'No!!!' The keeper had saved it, but quick as a flash, Alonso slammed home the rebound—amazing. I was standing there in front of a little TV in utter disbelief, watching my team come back from 3-0 down and now just one goal away from winning the Champions League final—was I watching the greatest match ever to be seen?

Thirty minutes to go, and I am frantically pacing backwards and forwards, hoping, praying and, at last, believing that Liverpool could get another goal to secure victory. Rafa stands on the pitch, talking to the players, probably telling them what every other Liverpool fan, and every other decent football supporter in the world who wanted to see that trophy come back to English soil, was thinking: 'Go on, push forward and take any chances that come our way!' Extra time kicked off, the nervous tension increased even further and we all knew whichever team scored next would surely lift the cup. As every minute passed, it became more and more apparent that we were heading for penalties—and that time duly arrived. As both teams lined up on the halfway line, the keepers getting themselves ready for the most important moment of their footballing careers, I stood there in front of that TV and watched history unfold—clapping at every AC Milan miss and screaming so loud when Liverpool scored that uninterested bystanders in the lounge bar knew exactly what was going on.

In the space of two hours, I had forgotten all about my personal troubles—even that my grandad was no longer with us—but to this day, I believe that my grandad was there at that stadium, willing Liverpool to win, standing behind the goal as AC Milan were taking their penalties and trying his best to put them off as best he could. I do like to think that this was his parting gift to me, to provide a bright moment in all that sadness in which we could all forget our troubles. I know that is what he would have wanted.

On the day of the funeral, I dressed in my Parade uniform and made sure my boots were so shiny they resembled a mirror. Grandad had served with the Green Howards, so I knew he would have been proud to have seen me dressed like that. When we got to the church, my brother, Barry, my uncles, Michael and John, and I went to the hearse where my grandad was laid in his Union Jack-draped coffin, and the four of us carried him into the church. As he was on my shoulder, I looked at his coffin and said in a low, quiet voice, 'Thank you for last night, grandad, I love you, until we meet again.' I will never forget those two days. They brought me emotions on two very opposite sides of the spectrum, yet underlined why I will continue to support Liverpool until my dying day.

Mark Newton *pictured on previous page, serving in Afganistan*

ALL ABOARD

On 17 August 1964, a football match took place in Reykjavik, Iceland, which was to be the precursor for many European nights for Liverpool Football Club. What was even more significant was that the journey to Iceland had been made by many Liverpool supporters. One fan's journey, however, was not made by charter plane (which cost an arm and a leg at the time) but by hitchhiking and then by fishing trawler.

This type of ingenuity was to set the precedent for the next 40 to 50 years for the way in which Liverpool fans, despite financial constraint, will overcome any obstacle to support their team. Even today, going to Europe to watch the Reds has become a rite of passage for many young men and one that many look forward to from an early age. But here is the story of Peter Smith.

Peter, born in 1935 and now 75 years of age, was 28 at the time and a regular, along with eight friends, on the Spion Kop. He recalled: 'It was after the win against Arsenal when we won the League that we all decided that, whoever we drew in Europe, we would make a holiday out of it and go and watch the Reds abroad.' Unfortunately Liverpool drew Reykjavik, and the desire to watch Liverpool's first European away game soon evaporated, despite the pledge.

But the fact that everyone else had given up the dream hardened Peter's resolve: The ex-armed forces man set about planning his trip to Iceland and took advice from local seamen from Ellesmere Port. The advice he got was to make his way to Hull, go to the shipping office and try and get on a trawler bound to Iceland. His friends and family thought he was 'stark raving mad'! After the pub, Peter set off at 10pm with £20 in his pocket on 7 August, allowing 10 days to get to Iceland. He hitchhiked from Ellesmere Port to Hull through the night, arriving at 7:30am, where he made his way to the shipping office as suggested, and they put him in touch with the crew of a trawler called Nathan that was bound for Reykjavik.

The captain was flabbergasted that someone would want to go all the way to Iceland for a football match, but nevertheless agreed that Peter could come aboard if he could work his passage, so he agreed to work in the galley on the outward voyage. The crossing would take between four and six days, depending on the weather. In the end it took five days.

Luckily, the work in the galley was well within Peter's capabilities, and he thought everything was ok, until one night at about 2am when he was woken from his bunk and issued with some oilskins and then told to report on deck. As he emerged on deck, Peter discovered that the trawler was in the middle of an ice storm, and the wind and cold were so extreme that the spray from the sea was building up as ice on the boat. Peter was given a 100m^2 area to clear using an axe; then, when he'd finished, he had to start chipping away at the ice all over again. This went on for many hours, and he recalls, 'It was adrenaline that kept me going; fatigue was overcome by the fear that the boat would capsize if we didn't break the ice from the boat. I have never been so wet and cold in all my life!' Peter added: 'The boat didn't start fishing 'til after it had reached Icelandic waters, but the lads worked very hard getting all the nets ready.'

On the fifth day, the trawler docked in Reykjavik harbour, and Peter was told, in no uncertain terms, that if he wanted a lift back to England, then he must be at the quay when the boat docked. Peter recalls: 'I was told they wouldn't wait, and they wouldn't send anyone to look for me. So I had to report to the local fishing office every day to see when my trawler was due in.'

When he disembarked from the trawler, he was taken to a local pub by members of the crew, some of whom had been visiting Reykjavik for years. It was in the pub that he was introduced to some locals who had their very own Liverpool supporters club—many being ex-seamen who had stood on the Kop while their ships where docked in Liverpool. They had been tipped off by the crew that they had some mad Liverpool supporter on board who was coming over for the match! Peter was befriended by numerous people, and the pub became his base. When it was closing time, he found himself being taken back to various houses so he could sleep and be fed. He had become quite a local celebrity.

On the day of the match, a lot of the Icelandic people wanted to meet Peter and to shake his hand, and after paying at the gate to get in, he was very surprised to see how many other Liverpool fans from Merseyside had made the journey, too.

The following is an account of the players' and staff's 'tortuous' journey to Reykjavik. If only they knew what Peter had endured out in the North Atlantic!

'On the morning of 16 August 1964, Ron Yeats, Ian Callaghan, Roger Hunt and company clambered aboard a coach outside Anfield, thus beginning a European odyssey, which, more than 40 years on, is unrivalled in the British game.

The Reds' first port of call, after finally subscribing to continental football, was Iceland. If you thought getting to Istanbul was tortuous, it was nothing compared to what Bill Shankly's League champions had to endure to play their first European Cup match.

After boarding a plane at Speke Airport, the squad flew first to London, then Glasgow, before eventually taking off for Reykjavik.

No wonder they got off to a "flying" start when kick-off finally arrived. Three minutes in, reserve forward Gordon Wallace scored Liverpool's first goal in continental competition. Four more followed on the night, and a 6-1 demolition at Anfield secured an 11-1 aggregate win. Not a bad start...'

Thankfully Peter did find out when the trawler was due in and, to his relief, was there ready and waiting at the quay. This time, though, he wasn't in the galley. He was given a job down below, gutting the fish! Understandably, 'I have never been so ill in my life; I had to slice open the cod with a knife and remove the guts with my hands. There was all sorts of fish, big skate and everything.' Peter made it home five days later, having been away for 17 days in total, and, if football fans received medals, Peter would have earned himself the equivalent of the Victoria Cross. Instead, however, as it happened, he got the sack from his job.

When Liverpool played the return leg, three Icelandic people stayed in Peter's house in Little Sutton, Ellesmere Port, for three days. Peter recalls, 'I took them on the Kop, and everyone was great with them. In fact, the Kop that night ended up cheering and supporting Reykjavik—the crowd were ecstatic when the Icelandic team scored!'

Having supported Liverpool all over Europe with little or no money, I can understand the me
of this proud and resourceful man, and I am extremely proud to have spoken to a fan that
should go down in Liverpool fan folklore.

Tony Kelly *pictured with Peter on p. 35*

CAMPIONI, CAMPIONI

On a recent trip home, my older brother took out some old, dated photos taken on our trip to Rome in 1984 for the European Cup final to see the Reds take on Roma in their own stadium... Gulp! In the photo, not only am I 26 years younger, but my hair is completely black and curly. I am also wearing a stupid red and white cap, while my 'stylish', classic Adidas T-shirt looks more orange than red as the photo has faded over the years. There was also one of me waving a flag in front of my dad's old Citroen Ami 8. The trip involved me, my brother Rob and my 'mate' Gary, who was not one of my usual acquaintances. He was a decent enough lad, at 19 he was a year younger than me, but also one of those friends forced on you by your parents. You know the sort of relationship—my parents were friends with his parents, so therefore we must be buddies. In truth, we didn't have that much in common, and I always thought he was a bit of an odd one—but enough of that! My brother had been to Rome in '77 and Wembley in '78, so he had been lucky to have been there to see two of our previous three European Cup wins. Gary and I were virgins when it came to European Cup finals. The tickets for Paris in '81 were rarer than a Manchester United title in those days, so that trip was a non-starter.

Of course, 1983/84 had been an epic season: Liverpool had already clinched the title and won the League Cup for the fourth time in a row after beating Everton in a replay at Maine Road and had played a colossal 66 matches, using just 15 players during the campaign. But the European Cup would be the icing on the cake, and we were going! The trip took us first to Lime Street,

where we boarded the 'Football Special' to Rome filled with a mixture of emotions—we were nervous, excited, enthused and anxious in equal measure. Lime Street station was filled with so many Liverpool fans; although, apparently, there weren't as many fans travelling compared to 1977, largely due to rumours of planned attacks by Roma fans that put a lot of Liverpool fans off travelling. The fact that tickets were very hard to come by because the Romans snapped up any that came available in their own stadium also kept many fans away. There were around 500 fans on each train that pulled out of Lime Street in convoy, and, as we headed south towards Runcorn, some fans got the singing under way, while others got stuck into playing cards or, of course, the beer! As the train chugged its way south and we started to get to know some of the lads sitting near us, we regaled each other with various away-day stories and crazy drink-fuelled antics. My brother's tale of us getting legged at Villa Park in 1979 earned a particularly loud laugh. The usual banter ensued. My 'mate', Gary, who had blond spiky hair and fancied himself as a punk (he was about as punk as my 80-year-old mum), started receiving a fair amount of stick from some of the older heads, but, fair play to him, he gave as good as he got as we all started to gel—a travelling army, all together. Then an odd thing happened.

A couple of hours in, just south of Birmingham, I guess, one of the lads in our carriage decided to take his shoes and socks off. I've never forgotten the smell, and it hit us in a wave that smelt like someone had died, been decomposed then died again. Laughing at our disgusted reactions, the lad smiled, opened the sliding window and threw out his rancid socks, while the rest of us looked on incredulous. He then coolly opened up his holdall, tore off some plastic and pulled out a fresh white pair of tube socks. 'Don't worry lads, I've got loads more where that came from. Only a pound on Church Street!' He must have had about two dozen pairs stuffed in his bag, and, for the rest of the journey, every three hours or so, he'd go through the same ritual of lobbing his socks out of the window and putting on a new pair. Bizarre, but very funny! We finally made it to the ferry, but God knows where we sailed from! What I do know is that as soon as we were all on board, the beer really started flowing, and it wasn't long before some of the lightweights were in trouble and leaning over the side. Wisely, the three of us decided to take things easy, my older brother reminding us that we still had a long way to go. However, we did stand and toast the sight of the approaching French coast when it came into view. Then it started lashing down with rain, so we legged it inside.

On the train, of course, the Liverpool fans were all cocooned together, but on the ferry we were forced to mix with the general public, who you could tell weren't at all happy at the prospect, to say the least. Some wished us well, while others, with wild fear in their eyes, avoided us like the plague. A few of the more drunken souls got a bit tired of this attitude and started singing profanity-filled songs about eating their children and the like, which must have made the scared holiday-makers feel a whole lot more comfortable! Arriving in France—Cherbourg maybe, possibly Calais—we were quickly herded onto another train. Before we left the French port, the police and officials came through and did the obligatory passport check. A couple of smart alecks swapped passports to test out the French Gendarmes' sense of humour, and you could feel people's spirits lifting even more now that we were finally on foreign soil. We were well on our way, well lubricated and in good voice. I can still hear the renditions of 'We going to Italy, tell me ma me ma...' echoing along the carriages as the French train sped south towards the French—Italian border.

Some of the Liverpool police on board accompanied us the whole way, along with a British Rail conductor named George, which we all thought was a bit odd. But he was a great old fella, who kept walking through the train letting people know what time we would be at our next destination and what to look out for on the journey. A lot of the lads on the train had been abroad before, but for the likes of Gary, who was on his first trip outside of England (or without his mum and dad), it was a whole new adventure. I was quite used to travelling with my brother—just the year before we had gone all the way to Belgium for a Van Morrison concert! Jetsetters, eh!

Although we were staying on the same train, the Italian officials insisted on us all getting off the train while they searched when we reached the French—Italian border, but few fans complained as we were treated to a great view of the Alps and the weather was beautiful. In any case, it gave us all a good chance to stretch our legs and wander about a bit. Then, before getting back on, we all had to go through the passport check again, which is when the mood changed slightly. For some reason known only to the Italian police, George, our British Rail conductor, was pulled to one side and not allowed back on the train. Nobody was sure why, but there seemed to be some mutterings about whether he was authorised to travel with us in the first place after we had left England, but either way, and after a bit of a shouting match, he was frog-marched away by the Italians as another pair of stinking socks was lobbed out of the window in protest. The fans aboard were clearly not happy, though, and a hat was passed up and down the train to try and raise enough money to bribe the police. Negotiations for George's release obviously failed, though, as we finally pulled off without him.

As we inched our way towards Rome, and through some fairly nondescript parts of Italy, the songs started coming thick and fast, and more and more of our chatter turned to the crucial match ahead. Who were their danger men? Who would our starting 11 be? The second question was far easier to answer as our team had been amazingly consistent all season: Grobs, Neal and Kennedy at full-back, Lawro and Hansen in the middle. In midfield, Souness, Whelan, Lee and Craig Johnston. My favourite was Johnston as I admired his energy and commitment, but, from listening to the others, some clearly didn't want him in the team. Up front was one of the best pairings on the planet, then or now: Rush and Dalglish. If I remember rightly, Rushie had scored 47 goals in all competitions that season—unbelievable!

The consensus of opinion was that Roma's main danger came from a couple of Brazilians and two Italians. Falcao and Cerezo, the two Brazilians, were our big worry, especially Falcao. Liverpool's speed at the back wasn't well regarded, and although Barney Rubble (Alan Kennedy) was a crowd favourite, he wasn't very quick. The two Italians, Conti and Pruzzo, were also scary prospects. We all agreed that Hansen and Lawro could handle the latter, but height was certainly a threat. Conti was the bigger worry—quick, skillful, unpredictable. There were also some grumblings about playing the final on their home pitch. 'It should be neutral', some moaned, while the conspiracy theorists claimed it was a fix to stop all the English teams repeatedly winning the trophy during the late 70s and early 80s. Then, after 24 very long hours, in which time I honestly don't recall sleeping at all, we arrived in Rome.

The Italian police greeted us at the train station and herded us onto buses bound straight to the Olympic Stadium. It was clear there was no time for sightseeing, other than out of the bus windows! In any case, there were now only about two hours until kick-off. We were let off a little before the stadium to wander the streets—some took a dip in the fountains, others bought pizza slices from street vendors. I can still clearly recall bowling past the Coliseum and on towards the Olympic Stadium with our flags and banners unfurled, as other groups of Liverpool fans merged with us. What a feeling!

Liverpool fans gathered together and belted out our anthems and snapped up overpriced pennants and flags from the hawkers before heading inside the cavernous stadium, which seemed nothing like an English football ground. The wide-open bowl was already filled with Roma fans letting off flares and waving banners. It seemed a sea of darker red. Suddenly we realised what a home advantage they had. Just think of a Cup final held at Anfield! We'd win every time, even with Avi Cohen in the team.

We found a decent position on the terracing and admired the lovely barbed wire that surrounded us and the submachine gun toting Italian police and their snarling, ferocious dogs. It was certainly not Prenton Park, and one of only a few occasions where the travelling Kop was being out-sung. It wasn't surprising really, bearing in mind that there were 80,000 Italians and only 10,000 or so Kopites; however, that would change as the match unfolded. The match kicked off, and we soon witnessed the Italians' ability to keep the ball and play possession football—not to mention the flares, fireworks and noise from their boisterous fans. We knew very early on this was going to be no picnic. However, Graeme Souness slowly got a grip in midfield, and it was the Mighty Reds who carved out and took the first chance of the match. My hero, Craig Johnston, got down the right wing and whipped in an awkward cross. Ronnie Whelan pressured their goalie and defender, and, even though the action was taking place at the far end of the stadium, the traveling Reds, peering through the smoke from the flares, were able to see Phil Neal (what on earth was he doing there?) get his second European Cup final goal, banging it into the empty Rome net. Then chaos reigned!

We've all done it. We've all gone mad when Liverpool have scored in a Cup final, but live, in person, with 10,000 of your 'best friends' surrounding you, after 24 hours of traveling, all that pent up emotion was released, and WE WENT MAD! The celebrations carried on and on, as did the songs, which shut the Roma fans up no end. Roma did start to pressure more, and Conti in particular was looking dangerous. But their fans were getting impatient. They were expecting to give us a hiding at home, and never in their wildest dreams did they think they would be 1-0 down after just 15 minutes. However, as the first half was drawing to a close, the pressure began to build, and, after a couple of corners and a few close shaves, Pruzzo suddenly got free and looped a header over Grobs, which settled in the net right in front of us to make the score 1-1. Of course, it was now the Romans' turn to go potty, and, as the first half ended, their celebrations continued. It had been an even 45 minutes—Souness was majestic, Johnston a threat and although Kenny was a little quiet, Rushie was harassing their defenders.

Because they had scored just before half-time and the crowd was fired up, we expected an Italian onslaught after the break. Thankfully, it never materialised, and, as the action got under way again, Liverpool enjoyed some great possession with the likes of Whelan, Lee, Souness and Lawro coming into their own. At the back, Hansen had things locked down in the middle, while Rushie was pressing them whenever they tried to build from the back. There was the odd chance here or there, but no sitters, no remarkable saves; in fact we'd reached stalemate—two fantastic teams engaged in a chess match. Rushie was scaring the life out of them with his speed, but he was being man-marked by at least two players, as they knew that with his 40-odd goals that's where our winner would come from.

The match went into extra time, where I would say we had most of the play. Souness was controlling the midfield with tough tackles but also great passing and vision. But to penalties it went. By then, Stevie Nicol had come on as sub, and we were surprised that he was chosen to take the first spot-kick, which he subsequently missed. Disaster. Tears started rolling down my face as anguish started to tie my emotions in knots. The 'defeat' word had crept into my head! But then the Italians blew it. Unnerved by Grob's antics, two Italians missed, and it was left for Barney Rubble to repeat his Paris heroics by scoring the winning penalty!

The relief, the joy, Souness with the cup—the rest is a blur. Coming out of the stadium, we were herded onto the buses again, only to be bombarded by the Italian scooter boys who threw petrol bombs, and a load of other things, at our bus windows, which shattered under the onslaught. Thankfully there was no hanging around, and the Italian police escorted us to the train station, and, less than five hours after we'd arrived in the Italian capital, we were back on the trains and headed homeward. The wild celebrations aboard the train are a vivid memory. The joy! The exultation! We had beaten them in their own backyard! 'Campioni! Campioni!' was sung over and over again, and none of us seemed to get tiring of it. And then, as we looked up, guess who was on the train? George, the conductor! Somehow he'd got to the match after explaining his situation and rejoined us for the journey home. I am sure the lads who passed the hat had pocketed the money, though, but nobody seemed to really care.

The singing and celebrations went on for hours as we wound our way north and out of Italy. We finally made it to the French coast and onto the ferry, which we drank dry—literally, there was not a drop to be had of any description. For some reason, we stopped briefly in London on the way back, and everybody jumped off the train to buy papers to read match reports. It was Friday morning by this stage, and stories of the team touring Liverpool the day before worked their way through the carriages, which annoyed a lot of fans who wanted to be back home and join in with the open-topped bus celebrations. 'Oh well', I thought, 'we were there!' Fatigue was kicking in, and I was beginning

to really struggle, but once we'd gone through Runcorn, everyone livened up for the final leg. All the flags and banners were re-hung out of the train windows, and the songs hit full volume again as everybody craned out of the windows, desperate for the first glimpse of home. Fellow Reds fans were waving at us from both sides of the tracks, and my dad (who has been gone for six years now) claims to have heard the songs for at least 10 minutes before the train arrived when he was waiting for us on the platform. 'I could hear you singing from Runcorn', he said proudly. We were finally home, and I'd seen us win the European Cup. Campioni indeed!

Mark Adams

THOSE WERE THE DAYS

Those were the days, my friends. New Year's Day, 1977, will be a date forever etched in my memory. Yes, it was my first match at that mythical place called Anfield. I was only eight, and although I had been surrounded by relatives who had talked about Shankly this and Inter that, Anfield was a place I had only seen on telly. Those misty European games shown on *Sportsnight* on a Wednesday night (with the floodlights along the top of the Kemlyn), or a few snatched minutes on Match of the Day, had elevated this ground, this cathedral, if you like, this place of worship, to an almost heavenly level in my young head. We won that day, 2-0 against Sunderland, with goals from Ray Kennedy and Phil Thompson and almost 45,000 fans packed into Anfield. I had never been at an event where so many people had gathered before, all wanting the same thing: a Liverpool win. It was the start of a love affair that, like any marriage, would have its highs and lows.

It was in the days before all-ticket demands, so it was essential to get to the ground early, or you simply wouldn't get in. Funnily enough, it was my dad who used to take me to the match in those early days, God bless his soul. He was an outsider—very much the OOT (if I can utter that acronym without getting into a 20-page debate) in our family. Born and bred a stone's throw

from West Ham's Boleyn Ground, my dad met my mum while on shore leave in Liverpool, and, like they say, the rest was history. He never even liked football much, but he must have seen the red tint in my eyes even at that age. He'd work his hard shift in Halewood all week and then take me to the match on Saturday morning—it was morning when we left, just to be sure we'd get in—while carrying a crate for me to stand on behind the goals in the Anny Road end. To go to the loo meant ducking under everyone's legs and coming up at the top for air, then trying to remember where you were standing. My second game came a few weeks later, at home to Carlisle in the FA Cup, and I ventured onto the Kop for my first taste of the tribalism and passion aboard the most famous terracing in the world. It was a bit of an accident ending up right at the very back, mainly because of the queues outside pushed us all the way past the Kemlyn and, with rumours of it nearly being a sellout, we entered at the nearest turnstile we could.

The Kop was a mass of people—a frightening but nevertheless fascinating place for an eight-year-old holding his dad's hand and cheering on the first Kevin Keegan goal he was to witness. It was virtually the same side that would go on and triumph in Rome at the end of that season and turn my young tears of despair after losing to Manchester United in the FA Cup final the Saturday before into tears of joy. Running around the estate I lived on with my friends holding aloft a homemade European Cup for about half an hour after the match is a wonderfully vivid memory still.

My match day experience involved going into a smoky pub for a pre-match chat—in some I had to stay outside, in others I could sneak in the corner—where I'd be handed a bag of chips. The pub seemed to have a working-class environment, a place where men let their hair down for a few hours on a Saturday. I'm not sure if the unwritten rule was that no women were allowed at football, but the ladies in my family were always left back at my nan's house on Queens Drive, awaiting the return of the troops from the battleground of Anfield. They always had their fingers crossed that we'd won, else the men would return with 'the cob on', as my nan always put it. I soon realised how critical the difference between winning or losing was and how the match result could make or break not only the rest of our family's weekend, but also the mood in the house the following week, too.

As I got older, I was allowed to go to the match on my own or with my mates, and, as we were too young to get in a boozer, we'd head straight for the kids' turnstile. Then, as we got older, we risked the dreaded tap on the shoulder from a local bizzy who'd instruct us to join the adults queue, which was usually five times longer and, of course, more expensive. We'd always keep a portion of the ticket stub that was ripped off at the turnstile and save them for derby match or big cup tie allocations, but there was always the odd scally asking to buy ticket stubs off you the moment you walked through the gates.

We always tried to stand in the middle of the Kop. The trick was to get a spot just in front of a barrier so that when the mass movement occurred, you didn't get squashed and bring up most of your pre-match chips! The stand held around 20,000 people, and the noise generated was deafening. The sway was actually scary at times. Even though it held so many people, you still spotted the same faces near your 'spec'. There were times when you couldn't even see the action as you were pushed to one side, then pushed back again, then down the Kop. But everyone

seemed to look after everyone else—Liverpool were a team on and off the pitch. If you fell, somebody was there to pick you up, which was mirrored on the pitch. Songs were about winning this, drinking that, fighting them—a working-class, shop-floor, hairy-arsed docker mentality.

In those pre-internet, pre-Sky days, fans didn't know the names of the board of directors or details about the owners. It didn't matter who was running the club as the team were playing so well and winning things. Anfield had become the fortress that Shanks built, and Paisley had continued to strengthen. It was a place to be feared both on and off the pitch. The opponents came with as much trepidation as the opposing fans. It was a working man's game, a place for a release from the hard working life they endured, if they were lucky to even have a job.

As we moved out of the post-Heysel days, the need for cash to keep up with our domestic and European rivals started to change the atmosphere and match-going experience. It didn't happen overnight, but there was a slow evolution over a number of years, which we should have seen coming the day they opened a McDonald's at the back of the Kop. The Sky revolution has totally changed the match-going experience, and saturation level is available in the houses of most people. Previously, football was a lifestyle choice or for those who had seen the baton passed down from generation to generation. Families previously not interested in the game have started showing an interest. The make-up of Liverpool's crowds is no longer almost exclusively working-class men with like-minded mates. Women no longer wait at home, hoping their men return home happy—they have joined the Red Army, too. Football became safe, however: the excitement, that 'edge', that... special something has been lost from our wonderful game forever. In fact, perhaps going to football has become too nice. There is a balancing act within the game, not just at Liverpool; yes, we need an environment of total safety where tragedies like we witnessed at Hillsborough are never repeated, but we also need a certain degree of edginess, too. We need to hate losing again, just like when the working men gathered in the smoky post-match pubs, dreading going back into work on the Monday morning. Not just complaining about how hot the pies are, or if someone has stood up in their way, or leaving 10 minutes before the end of the match to catch their plane home. Football seems to be more about the experience than the result to an ever-growing section of the crowd. Before I set off to the match, my wife always says to me, 'Enjoy!' and my reply is always the same, 'Never mind enjoy... I want to win!'

And I want to win every game badly, just like my brother does, just like my uncle did, just like my grandad did, and his dad before him. Maybe I'm looking back through red-tinted specs, but I long to return to the days when we were a team on and off the pitch.

Nick Harman

WE ARE A FAMILY

'You'll Never Walk Alone' became more than just words when I lived through some of my darkest hours. Growing up in a household that consisted of a grandad who loved Liverpool and a nanna who had a curious love for Brazil, football was never off the menu. I remember the shouting from my grandad and my nanna telling him to behave—it was a truly passionate football household. However, in 2003 my nanna became terminal ill. I felt lost and alone. I would try anything to detach myself from the world, but nothing helped. When my nanna was sent to the hospice, we all knew that time was limited. I would stare out of the window, hoping that something would give me strength. That something, anything, would remind me that I was not alone in this. While in the hospice, Liverpool played Manchester United on 5 April 2003. I decided to miss the match, to go and spend time with my nanna, but when my grandad arrived at the hospice, after watching the game at home, he told me that the final score was 4-0. At that moment, I knew that if a miracle could not happen for Liverpool, it would not happen for my nanna. Just a few days after my nanna's death, I felt lost, and even throwing myself into schoolwork and hobbies did not help. I felt totally alone. However, after talking to some Liverpool fans, I realised that I was not alone. That we were not just connected through our love for Liverpool, but through so much more. Therefore, this story is a thank-you to all the Liverpool fans out there. We may bicker, moan and argue among ourselves. We may have our disagreements and, at times, we annoy each other, but that is because we are a family! Thank you for letting me be a part of you and for being not just supporters but friends. Thank you for not letting me walk alone.

Danielle Haigh-Wood

RED
STARS
IN THEIR
EYES

In 1981, I had to go to Leningrad for work and, to my horror, was forced to miss the European Cup final in Paris. Obviously my three Scouse colleagues and I were determined not to miss out on the game completely, but we were dismayed to find that not only was the game not being televised in Russia, but also that long wave radios were banned in Russia. This meant that the hotel staff would not allow us to listen to the radio we had brought along with us specially on their premises, and we were forced to go wandering the streets with it instead.

The desperate situation led to four Kopites roaming hopelessly around the city with our trusty wireless, trying to keep up to date with the action in the French capital. Our actions obviously looked suspicious, though, because we were quickly stopped by a police patrol car. The officers demanded to know what we were doing. We were threatened with arrest and told that we had committed all sorts of crimes against the state.

We explained, as best we could, that we were desperate to find out information from the European Cup final, and, eventually, they seemed happy with our explanation—until they noticed our scarves, hats and flag. After confiscating our precious Liverpool stash, they finally seemed happy to let us go on our way.

To add insult to injury, just as we were crossing a bridge across the River Neave, Barney Rubble scored for the Reds, which triggered wild scenes of jubilation among the four of us. However, the person holding the radio lost his grip as we jumped around and hugged each other, and we all stood open-mouthed as the radio left his hand and plunged into the river below.

It took us another four hours to successfully phone home from our hotel, but we eventually discovered that we had won. In fairness to the rest of the guests in the hotel, they were quite happy to join in our celebrations, even though it was 3am by that stage!

Alun Thomas

THANKS TO KEN

It was the spring of 1979 in Denmark, I was 11 years old, and my mother was talking about her birthday, which is 14 April. She said that she wanted to go to England to see Liverpool to celebrate. So we checked the match calendar, and that day the Reds were playing Manchester United! We had never been to Liverpool, but we were optimistic as we packed the car, took the ferry across and checked into the Liverpool center hotel, which today is called The Liner, I think. On match day, we got up, and my brother and father immediately went to Anfield to look for tickets on sale. My mother and I followed by taxi later.

It was while we were driving to Anfield that the taxi driver asked us where we were from and if we had tickets for the big

game. My mother said we were from Vordingborg in Denmark and that we had no tickets. He said that the game had sold out long ago, but if we wanted, we could try the Liverpool office at Anfield and ask for a man called Ken Addison. Maybe he could help us, said the driver.

My mother thanked him for his advice, and, after doing as instructed, a well-dressed man came to the counter, looked at us strangely and asked what he could do for us. My mother explained that it was her birthday and that we had come from Denmark to see the game but had no tickets!

Mr Addison said that everything had sold out long ago, but then paused for a second before adding, 'Just a minute.' He went to his office and, to our delight, came back with four tickets, saying, 'Here are the tickets which me and my family should have used today, but I want you to have them so that you can watch the game after coming all the way from Denmark on your birthday!'

We were totally blown away by this gesture and thanked him as warmly as we could. We then went into Anfield for the very first time. With the sun shining down, we sat in the front row with all the directors and watched Liverpool beat United 2-0! What a wonderful day, what a wonderful man, what a wonderful club. Our family has supported Liverpool with all our hearts ever since.

Later that year, we sent some Royal Danish china as a thank-you gesture to Ken Addison, and, believe it or not, Ken invited my father, who was a football coach at the time, over to be an official guest at the club for a week! So, in December 1979, my dad returned to watch a game, to view the training, to meet Bill Shankly and Bob Paisley and, possibly the icing on the cake, to enjoy a post-match whiskey with Graeme Souness. What wonderful memories from a wonderful football club.

Mads Herholdt

A STITCH IN TIME

It was the day of the Champions League final in Istanbul, but I couldn't have been farther away from the action. I was off travelling and working on Hamilton Island, close to the Great Barrier Reef in Australia, at the time and living with an Australian girl. We'd made a lot of Ozzie mates on the island who, on the big day, were only interested in the State of Origin rugby match game where their leagues' top players turn out for one of the four states in a kind of play-off showdown. Obviously I didn't give a stuff in this odd-ball affair, and I hadn't waited up until 4am to watch the Reds' progress at every Champions League stage to miss the big one, so I made plans for the day.

A group of us got together for a boozy day, which included watching their rugby game, before my girlfriend and I headed back to her place at about 11pm to carry on the party. I told her I was taking no risks and set my alarm just in case we nodded off, which we duly did at around 1:30am. The alarm went off just as the match kicked off, so we both refilled our glasses and settled into watching the game. Obviously at 3-0 down, I was dismayed and my beer intake escalated accordingly, but somehow, for some reason, I still had faith in the Reds, even when my girlfriend said, 'I don't know much about football, but it's not looking good for Liverpool.' At that stage, it would have been so easy to just switch the TV off and go to bed, but I replied, 'We never give up, just you watch!' And I can remember jumping around with joy and roaring on the boys as the first two goals went in, and then, to our amazement, we levelled the scores.

At this stage, I was very drunk yet still alert, probably from the adrenaline that was pumping through me having watched arguably the best comeback the footballing world has ever seen. But then disaster struck. As the penalty shootout reached its stunning finale, like all Reds I was barely able to keep a lid on my emotions when Dudek saved a shot from Shevchenko. And, as I jumped into the air, my bare foot landed on my pint glass, and, in an instant, the whole floor was covered in blood. At the precise moment I should have been celebrating like never before, my girlfriend was screaming with shock and fear. At first I thought it was just a flesh wound, but she was sober enough to know it was bad and rang her brother, who lived on a houseboat on the bay. He rushed over in a speedboat to assess the damage—basically, there was a three-inch laceration under my right ankle, which had opened up as wide as my mouth.

After hearing all the screams at our place and thinking there was a serious domestic dispute in progress, our neighbours had called the island's security team, which was a blessing in disguise because we were simply unable to stop the flow of blood. After seeing the carnage for themselves, the security men quickly put me in their jeep and dashed toward the medical centre, where I started singing victorious Liverpool songs. The doctor tried to stitch my wound up, but, as it kept opening back up, he decided to use fishing line until I could be brought to the mainland to get a proper job done on it. As the sun started to rise, I was still singing even though there was talk about getting a helicopter to fly me to the nearest hospital. I had hit an artery under my right ankle and had lost more than a pint and a half of blood. The medical staff told me that I could have bled to death, but all I cared about was my beloved Reds lifting the cup.

It was the great Bill Shankly who said football was more important than life and death. Never have truer words been said, because I almost died that night, and because my accident is so much part of my memory of Liverpool winning the Champions League, I wouldn't change a thing, despite the large scar.

David McCluskey *pictured left with his son*

THE JOY AND PAIN OF SAINT-ÉTIENNE

Of course, back in 1977, Liverpool had not quite established its awesome reputation in Europe. The League Championship win in 1975/76, then again the following year, proved the team were a major domestic powerhouse, but the European Cup was another thing altogether. It was still a time when we Liverpool supporters knew comparatively little about teams from across the channel; however, call it slightly naive, we were convinced that European glory was the destiny of the lads in red. Because of our anticipation for European glory, these ties were looked forward to with huge excitement on Merseyside—and probably none more so than the visit of the French champions, Saint-Étienne, that March evening in 1977. The fact that the opposition were French and it was the latter stages of the European Cup was more than enough to set the adrenaline pumping. To add to the excitement, Liverpool were a goal behind from the first leg to a team with a mean defence and a potent attack. How my mates, Steve Baker and Neil Crumpton, and I got tickets for the match is still beyond me—the feat would be almost impossible today—as we were all mates from Liverpool University, and I was the only Liverpool supporter among us.

My love affair with the club borders on the irrational. It started when I was 10 because I liked the sound of Liverpool—maybe it had something to do with the pop culture, I don't know—but in those days the Reds were no great shakes, so I can't be accused of being a glory hunter. Living in Southampton, some 200 miles away, meant that I'd never been to Anfield, but I would religiously visit The Dell for the Liverpool game where I'd invariably see my heroes lose—even in the days of

Lawler and Larry Lloyd. So, when the chance came for me to be able to publically demonstrate my allegiance to the club, I took it with both hands. That opportunity came when I had to select my university and course when I reached 18. At the time I was devoted to the study of marine biology—Jacques Cousteau and Hans Hass vying for my loyalty along with Toshack and Keegan—and the only universities to offer such a course were Aberystwyth, Bangor and, thank goodness, Liverpool. So, I can truly say that when I received my A-level results, the major deciding factor for which university I went to was not the quality of the course, but the quality of the football teams. Need I say more? At that time, the city of Liverpool had everything: The team were starting the era of true dominance and pop groups were visiting the Empire and Stadium all the time, including the likes of Yes, Queen, Status Quo and Bad Company. There seemed to be a real sense of excitement around the city.

So, there we were on that evening in '77, tickets in hand and entering the very sanctum of football—the middle, yep, dead centre, of the all-standing, all-singing, all-famous Kop. An hour

before kick-off, and the atmosphere was electric. It was like nothing I'd ever witnessed. Everywhere I looked, people were chanting and waving red flags, you know, the big ones that descend upon you like an eclipse of the sun. Where do they get those things and how do they bring them into the crowd? And all our idols were there: Clemence, Toshack, Kennedy (ok, perhaps he wasn't yet an idol but what a footballer he was already) and, of course, everyone's favourite after scoring on his debut and sporting that crazy hairdo, Kevin Keegan. One goal down but all to play for.

The scene was set for an amazing rendition of 'You'll Never Walk Alone', and it was duly delivered with stratospheric emotion. The toss went Liverpool's way, and, for the first 80 seconds, the match was even! Then, amazingly, Keegan scored from the left wing. Now some say it was a clever chip, but I've always believed that it was a cross ball that a higher being (yes, even higher than Kevin) saw fit to blow into the net. Who cares! We had levelled the tie within the first two minutes; now Liverpool were really in the ascendancy. To be fair, Saint-Étienne were one helluva team, and no matter how the fans chanted, roared and swore, the Frenchmen held their own. It was not truly a shock when Bathenay scored with a great shot that even Ray Clemence had no chance with. My, we were in for a fight, no question.

The crowd's reaction was incredible: following a 60-second silence after the Liverpool net rippled, the realisation that we now needed two sank into each and every one of us, and Anfield rose as one. Flags were everywhere I looked, so many in fact that it felt that I was the only person who hadn't brought one. The Bathenay goal came early in the second half, so Liverpool had time and when Ray Kennedy scored with 32 minutes still to go, Anfield simply went crazy again. I believe that there were some French supporters there, but you wouldn't believe it. Then, 26 minutes after Ray's goal, something happened that is forever entrenched in my mind.

For those of you who didn't stand on the Kop on such a night, I should perhaps describe a few things. Firstly, the steps were pretty steep. Secondly, when the ball came towards the Kop, the whole crowd moved forward, and you had to be nimble on your feet as you may have to navigate two, three or even more steps at a time just to keep standing. And thirdly, at strategic points, there were immovable metal barriers to curtail too much crowd swell. I'd noticed that confident and more experienced supporters often stood behind these barriers in the knowledge that when the ball came forward they had time to get their leg up onto the metal and save themselves from being pushed down several flights of stairs. An interesting possibility, I thought. Now, I was confident alright, but unfortunately not experienced. Even so, after several buffetings, I decided to move behind a barrier, smack bang in the middle of the Kop, and things were fine for a while. If I could get my leg up in time, I'd be fine... if only!

Well, with six or so minutes to go, Kennedy snatched the ball back from a tired Saint-Étienne player somewhere in midfield and played a quick pass forward. Now, some say this was a defence-splitting pass and, it's true, it did split the defence, but it was a bit fortunate, too. The point was that the ball landed perfectly for our great super sub (it was an inspiration to bring him on in place of Toshack) to run onto and, as he surged into the penalty area, right under my nose, did I have time to get my foot up onto the barrier? No, I tried my left arm instead in what proved to be a very bad decision. Of course you all know that Fairclough slotted the ball into the net past a despairing Curkovic, but what you don't know is that the full weight of the Kop applied itself, not to my leg, but to my elbow and where my hand was trapped, and I let out a howl of pain as my wrist broke in two places. Now, a broken wrist is a very painful thing to experience in any circumstance but when you snap it in the middle of a baying and joyous mass of people on the Kop it's far worse, believe me. I went down big time and didn't even see the goal. Of course, sitting under the barrier, I had a good idea we'd scored what was certain to be the winner by the sheer reaction of the crowd.

Now, I could tell you that in those mad moments my fellow Liverpool supporters leapt to my assistance, protected me and helped me to my feet to join the celebrations—but that simply did not happen. They had much more important things to do than worry about my well-being. In fact, I took an accidental kicking, too, as I lay on the terrace and was in a pretty sorry state. Adrenaline helped mask the pain to a certain degree as I tried to get up using just one arm, but it proved impossible. So I just sat there like an idiot waiting for the end of the game, one of Anfield's finest in living memory. Of course, on a night like that, the crowd is too pumped up and jubilant to think about leaving; fans want those moments to last forever. So, for another 30 minutes, I sat there until my mates came to cart me off. I gingerly got to my feet holding my left arm in my shirt as shock started to set in, and I shivered uncontrollably. Well, far be it for me to spoil the fun for my mates so off we marched to the pub. I don't know which pub it was, probably Steve's favourite, the Cambridge up by the university, but, wherever it was, it did have a staircase and that's where I sat and downed two pints of beer in very quick succession, which helped ease the pain a great deal. But regardless of the numbing values of lager, my arm was getting very swollen and very blue, and the little bone that's normally protruding on the outer side of your wrist was now underneath my wrist and looking very sorry for itself.

So, there we were, three reasonably intelligent students, faced with a rather difficult decision: carry on drinking or take me to the hospital. I'm glad Steve made the right call. I can only guess what time we arrived at Liverpool Hospital—positive it was pretty late—but a doctor looked at my arm almost straight away. It looked like I was in for a long night, so he sent my mates away, saying there was nothing more they could do. Off I went for an X-ray; it showed a double fracture, and it was clear that an operation was needed and that I would have to be completely knocked out for the task. Here lay a problem. You see, if you've had a couple of pints, no matter whether you enjoyed them or not, the doctors can't give you a general anaesthetic. Fair enough, I thought! So after a discussion with the doctor, where I admitted my visit to the pub, he bandaged my arm up and advised me to get a taxi home and to come back in the morning. That was another problem, as I had no money whatsoever.

You read lots of stuff about doctors being money grabbers or, occasionally, making huge, inexplicable blunders, but this guy was something else. After I told him I had no money, so I would have to sleep in a chair in the waiting room, he reached into his pocket, took out a tenner and just gave it to me. That is still a very fond memory—people just don't do that today, do they? Of course, I explained my

arm to the taxi driver, but he just thought I was a yob who had been in a fight after the match.

The night was not a comfortable one by any stretch of the imagination, so I was very pleased to get back to the hospital. I was given a nice cup of tea and, after a quick visit by a nurse, given my anaesthetic. I fancied a lovely university student who was studying nursing, so imagine my surprise when she entered the room to give me the injection. Now, if that wasn't a big enough shock, when she asked me to drop my pants, things became surreal. I thought those injections were done in your hand, but this one wasn't. And it was administered by a girl who I had many dreams about but had not even gotten close enough to kiss. Anyway, off I went into dreamland and woke, arm fixed, with a tray of tea and biscuits brought to me by another friendly university nurse who I also knew well. After my arm was plastered way above my elbow, I was released. I had brought money this time but, to my shame, never did pay the doctor back.

Trying to figure out Liverpool's most important comeback ever is an interesting pre-match discussion with your mates—Olympiakos and, of course, Istanbul come to mind—but what if we'd lost to Saint-Étienne? Would Liverpool have gone on to win all those European cups and league titles? It makes me think that maybe that game against the French was one of the most important wins in our proud history, and, for those lucky to have been there that night (unlike me!), it certainly won't be a painful memory!

Jon Page *with his daughter, Freja*

THE NIGHT SHIFT

My uncle, Tommy Donnelly, was a fanatical Red. He idolised the great Billy Liddell and would go and watch his beloved Liverpool whenever and wherever he could. Uncle Tommy was over the moon when Liverpool were eventually promoted to First Division in the spring of 1962, and it was not long after this momentous event, in September of '62, that the Reds were due to play their first top flight derby match against Everton at Goodison Park. It was by all accounts going to be a wonderful occasion—one that Tommy couldn't let pass without leaving his mark.

The night before the match, my uncle walked into his local pub, his hands covered in red paint. When my dad asked what he'd been up to, Uncle Tommy's answer was simple: 'You'll see in the Echo tomorrow!' He then laughed and bought a pint.

It transpired that on the eve of the match, my uncle and his friend had successfully completed a covert operation, which they had meticulously planned together. They had sneaked their way into Goodison Park and, under the cover of darkness, proceeded to paint the white goalposts a beautiful shade of Liverpool red! The 'expert' repainting of the goalposts was not noticed until the groundsman arrived the next morning. Unsurprisingly, the Evertonians were not very pleased with their new, 'improved' goalposts, and it was all hands on deck to restore them to their original colour—although

"RED" RAID ON GOODISON GOALS

Woodwork Painted

Liverpool supporters struck the first blow in the "derby" battle during the night. When the Everton ground staff arrived at Goodison Park this morning they found the two sets of goalposts had been completely covered with bright red paint.

Four men were immediately put to work scraping off the thick oil paint and rubbing down the posts with paint remover in a battle to restore them to their former pristine condition.

Said one of them: "There's no doubt who's responsible for this lot. They must have climbed into the ground about midnight last night. When we got here this morning the paint was completely dry.

FIRST IN THE QUEUE

Two 16-years-old Everton supporters were first in the queue at Goodison Park this morning.

Roy Wright, of 64 St. Anne Street, Liverpool, and Donald Walsh, of 12 Menai Road, Bootle, arrived at the Gladwys Street turnstiles at 9 p.m.

Two of the Everton F.C. ground staff, are scrapers and paint remover, strip the from the goalposts at Goodison Park be them in time for the kick-o

"REDS" WITHOU
ST. JOHN FOR T
DERBY GAME

it is rumoured that the paint was still wet when the game kicked off! But with security the way it is today, this heartfelt, unique display of devotion to the Reds would be nigh on impossible. There is a photo [previous page] of Uncle Tommy blowing the bugle he used to take to games. He would always travel to Anfield from Fazakerley and all the way back again squashed in the boot of his friend's car, and, after a Liverpool victory, he could be heard from far and wide, blowing the bugle in celebration as they all returned from the match. However, the family would fear the worst when the front door opened and there'd been no fanfare announcing his return, as that would usually mean there had been a Liverpool defeat. Sadly, Uncle Tommy is no longer with us, and our family misses him dearly.

Ali Maffitt

THE HEIGHWAY COED

In 1971, I was 16, living near Northampton and an ardent Liverpool supporter. I lived and breathed Liverpool as only a teenage girl could. My young neighbour, Mark, was an Arsenal supporter, so on Cup final day, I sent him a little note saying that my Reds would thrash his Gunners. BIG mistake. After the match, when I was already in a million bits of despair, Mark appeared at our doorstep with my note. He didn't say a word. He didn't need to. His face said it all. He simply ripped my note to shreds and let the pieces flutter to the ground. Oh, the humiliation! I cried like a baby.

At the end of the summer, my sister applied to a teacher training college in Liverpool, and I nobly offered to accompany her by train to the interview. Sisterly devotion? No, not quite. Before Jane's appointment, I dragged the poor girl to Anfield on a bus so that I could stand at the gates and gaze at the sign above the entrance. My sister didn't get her place; however, a year later, I'd completed my A-levels, and it was my turn to choose a university. Well, I say 'had to choose', but in truth there was no decision to be made really, even if the university's English and Philosophy joint honours course wasn't that highly recommended, academically speaking. Liverpool University was at the top of my list—way above Bristol and Edinburgh and Leeds. Neither Bristol nor Edinburgh nor Leeds met my requirements, not that I could see in the prospectus at any rate. They did not have Steve Heighway—or his moustache. Of course, I didn't mention that at my interview. I didn't know how well it would be received. I must have said the right thing—or rather, not said the wrong thing—because I got my place and spent four years at Liverpool. The happiest years of my life. The city of my dreams. The team of my dreams. The footballer of my... well, the less said about that the better. So, Steve Heighway and Liverpool Football Club, you are responsible for furthering my education, and I thank you for it!

Caroline Coxon

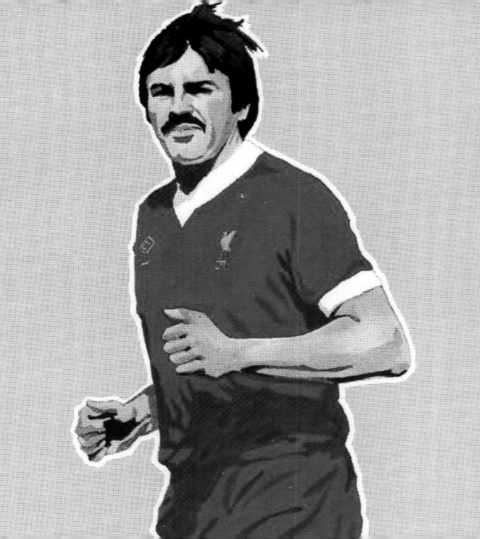

COPPA DEI CAMPIONI

SEMIFINALE

MILANO 12 MAGGIO 1965

SAN SIRO ore 21,15

INTER-LIVERPOOL

MY ITALIAN JOB

During the Shankly era, I worked as an Italian interpreter for the Liverpool Football Club squad when they travelled to Milan (1964/65) and Turin (1965/66), as well as for occasional home matches when the match officials were Italian. I accompanied Shankly as he moved about in Italy, for example when he went off looking for silk ties in Como, travelled with the directors and squad on the aeroplane or the team bus, and I actually sat beside the Liverpool legend on the bench during matches in Italy.

Whenever Shankly needed my services, I went where he went, including memorable official functions at the Jockey Club, where we 'enjoyed' a particularly hair-raising taxi ride. I also recall being awoken at about 3am by Mr Shankly one morning, who asked me to 'Silence those bells', which were preventing him from sleeping. In truth, these were not just any bells, but the church clock chiming the quarter-hours. Although, the locals did their best to keep the players awake during the nights, too, by circling the hotel on their scooters and cars, blowing their horns incessantly—and without police intervention. Other situations I assisted with included helping to solve the difficulty in obtaining fillet steaks in Milan, because Shankly insisted fresh, red meat was central to the players's diet, and an unforgettable coach ride from the hotel to the stadium, during which all the players, staff and directors sang 'You'll Never Walk Alone' all the way—what a morale booster! Not only did I sit on the bench during the matches in Milan and in Turin, but I also accompanied the Liverpool manager to the team dressing room at the half-time interval. I recall that in Milan there was a moat with a fence and very high bars, separating us from the passionate, howling mob of standing spectators, which was very intimidating. As we walked towards the dressing rooms at half-time, a bottle was thrown, which splintered at head height against the concrete wall just ahead of us. Thankfully no personal injuries were sustained on either side, although I remember an Italian player's shocked reaction when he said, 'Caspita!', meaning 'For God's sake!'

I'll always remember that during the 1964/65 semi-final second leg in the San Siro, Shankly was furious with the biased decisions of the Spanish referee, and I looked on as the Reds' manager sarcastically gave him a thumbs up sign, and shouted, 'Bene, referee!' In those days the club was still learning about playing in Europe. Liverpool had seen a 3-1 first-leg advantage turned on its head and witnessed firsthand how suspect decisions affected the outcome of matches. The powder-keg atmosphere may have caused much anger and frustration on the bench, but I was privileged to share those experiences with the legendary man.

Grattan Endicot

THE SPIRIT OF '93

During the 1993/94 season, I travelled from my home in West Sussex to watch Liverpool home and away games. As members of the LFC Supporters' Club London Branch, several friends and I made our way to matches by train or coach. On the pitch, it was not a good season. No European football and no silverware. The Graeme Souness reign was coming to an end, and the Roy Evans tenure was about to start. However, despite the lack of glory, I remember the season fondly. The camaraderie with fellow supporters and various trips that season live long in my memory, culminating in the Kop's last stand.

The season had started on a positive note. Liverpool put together three straight wins, including a Nigel Clough double against Sheffield Wednesday at Anfield on the opening day and away wins at QPR and Swindon Town. Coming back from Swindon, we felt positive about the season ahead, but it was a false dawn. By mid-September, cracks had started to appear, and a transfer market decision by Graeme Souness left us supporters baffled prior to the derby match with Everton. Julian Dicks had arrived from West Ham, with Mike Marsh and David Burrows going in the opposite direction. I remember the concerns of many supporters as we went around the pubs near Anfield and Goodison Park, searching for a spare ticket for one of our mates. The Reds went down 2-0 at Goodison, with Julian Dicks making his debut. A day to forget, especially the sight of Bruce Grobbelaar and Steve McManaman coming to blows.

One of the major positives from that season was the emergence of Robbie Fowler, and, following the defeat to Everton, Souness made changes. Robbie came in, scored and Liverpool ran out 3-1 winners in the League Cup at Fulham. It was a horrible, stormy night by the Thames, we were soaked to the skin on the open terrace, but Robbie's debut goal warmed our hearts. October gave us a late winner at home to Oldham, which taught me that I was right in never leaving a match before the final whistle. Two despondent mates left to catch an earlier train and missed the final drama. Another home win, 4-2 against Southampton, stands out, with the Kop applauding a Matt Le Tissier goal for the visitors. However, a Robbie hat-trick saw the Reds home.

November and December brought two poor away performances, resulting in defeats against Newcastle and Sheffield Wednesday. The Newcastle game stood out on a cold Sunday afternoon in the North East. One of our mates missed the Supporters' Club train at Kings Cross by seconds, but those of us who made it watched as Liverpool were taken apart by Beardsley, Lee and Cole. I remember standing in a corner of the open Gallowgate End, awaiting the final whistle and being bombarded by rather large hailstones. A positive memory from that day was sharing a pre-match pint with some Geordies who welcomed us to Newcastle in the name of football—if only all places could be the same.

December continued with a poor 2-2 draw against Swindon Town at Anfield, a game that the Premier League newcomers should have won. The Reds then lost to Wimbledon at Selhurst Park on penalties in the League Cup. Time was running out for Souness (in view of matters on and off the pitch), and some supporters had already had enough. It all culminated in the unprecedented 'Souness Please Go Now' flag at Spurs pre-Christmas. Following the 3-3 draw at White Hart Lane, we made our way to the London Branch Supporters' Club Christmas Social, hoping for better things from 1994.

Following the success of the 1980s, there is a school of thought that Anfield had become quieter, with silverware being taken for granted, but, in the 1993/94 season, I remember the support being fantastic both home and away. The supporters knew the team was struggling, and they had to carry them through a difficult time. I think the Liverpool support showed their true class, and I was proud to have been a part of that.

Supporters had organised Flag Days at Anfield during that final season of the standing Kop. One such night was 4 January 1994, against the then reigning League Champions, Manchester United. It left me with one of my final great memories of the old Kop. Having travelled to the game by coach, we met up for a pint at the Oakfield pub, our regular meeting place. The atmosphere in the ground was electric. The Kop was in great voice, and a friend in the Lower Centenary Stand caught on camera a red flare that was let off in the Kop pre-match. I remember a flag going over the heads of those around me, which was unusual because they never usually reached the back corner of the Kop where I stood. I also remember the passion in some of the more senior Kopites, who were singing and shaking their fists, willing the Red men to victory over their great rivals.

About 20 minutes into the game, we found ourselves 3-0 down. United, playing in an all-black away strip, were cruising, and I felt sick in my stomach. Then, Nigel Clough, playing probably his best game for Liverpool, scored two goals before half-time. Game on! We were back in it, and the Kop roared Liverpool forward. The equaliser, a header from Neil Ruddock, came late in the game, and Anfield exploded. A winner would have been the icing on the cake, but it was not to be. Sitting on the coach on the way home, I was proud to have witnessed such a great Liverpool comeback as, like other Reds, I knew our side were struggling, but the team had shown real passion and desire. We could ask no more. The following Saturday brought the third round of the FA Cup and a trip to Bristol City. The score was 1-1; Ian Rush was the Liverpool scorer, but, at 65 minutes, the floodlights failed following heavy rain, and the match was abandoned. It was bizarre situation, one I had not experienced before or since.

As January progressed, we went up to Oldham Athletic, catching a train journey from London, via Manchester, to Werneth Station, and walked through Oldham to Boundary Park. These away trips were always an education, and I remember being struck by the colourful shops and restaurants serving the local Asian community. We had a pre-match drink in the Eleven Ways pub, and, on a cold afternoon, I was kept going by a few pints of Guinness, but warmed by a 3-0 Liverpool victory. Julian Dicks, Robbie Fowler and Jamie Redknapp got the goals. A good day and a happy journey home.

January closed with Liverpool exiting the FA Cup, an injury to Robbie Fowler and the eventual departure of Graeme Souness. February opened with Roy Evans as manager and a trip to Norwich City, a game I remember for many reasons. Firstly, the relief that this was the start of a new era for the club, and there was total commitment to get behind the team and Roy in his first match in charge. Also, a good friend of mine had one too many pre-match; however, we managed to prop him up and get him past the stewards, and, in an attempt to disguise the smell of alcohol, I offered him a Fisherman's Friend. Oblivious to their industrial strength, he grabbed the packet and downed the lot—which was entertaining! The game ended 2-2, and Roy's reign was under way.

We enjoyed some banter with the Match of the Day commentator Barry Davies on the train back to London and discussed some talking points from the match, before he disappeared off down the train after being serenaded with 'There's only one Barry Davies' by my still drunk friend—a priceless memory. And then, on the London Underground, we bumped into Mark Lawrenson. We all shook Mark's hand, and I thanked him for all he had done for Liverpool as a player. He looked at me very strangely throughout, and I cringe when I think back to that meeting!

As winter turned to spring, Robbie Fowler returned for the Merseyside derby at Anfield, and Liverpool gained revenge—thanks to Rush's and Fowler's goals. I remember it being another Flag Day, and we took confetti to the game. As the teams came out, I launched it up towards the roof of the Kop, most of it coming down all over the lad in front of me. As he brushed it from his shoulders, his mate advised him that he may have some explaining to do to his wife later that evening.

The run-in to the end of the season was bleak: Defeats away to Arsenal at the end of March, Sheffield United at Anfield in early April and a tame 1-1 draw with Wimbledon at Selhurst Park highlighted the difficult job Roy had ahead of him. On Saturday 9 April, we caught an early train from London to see the morning kick-off at Anfield, with the Reds entertaining Ipswich Town on Grand National Day. The game was significant for two reasons: Liverpool's 1-0 win being the last home victory of the season and the goal, a Julian Dicks penalty, was the last goal scored by a Liverpool player in front of the old, standing Kop. At the end of the match, we headed off to Aintree for the horse racing and enjoyed the afternoon, watching Freddie Starr's Minnehoma win the National at 18-1. My mate won £190, and drinks were on him all the way home.

The following Saturday, Kevin Keegan brought his entertaining Newcastle United team to Anfield, and, like earlier that season, they ran out winners, this time 2-0. At the end of the game, Peter Beardsley, having acknowledged the travelling Newcastle support, turned to applaud and say farewell to the Kop, who responded in turn. I had a lump in my throat: Beardsley was a player I admired for his professionalism on and off the park, a player who left Liverpool far too early—another one of Souness' mistakes as far as I'm concerned. April closed with an away trip to West Ham United and the final home game against Norwich City. At West Ham, on a bright but cold spring afternoon, goals from Fowler and Rush gave Liverpool a 2-1 win. Then to The Kop's Last Stand on 30 April 1994.

The support, colour and noise that day was fantastic; the fans were a credit to the club. Reds fans brought out old scarves and banners from yesteryear. It was quite an occasion. As a child, I had watched on television as Liverpool won the European Cup in Rome in 1977 and marvelled at the travelling Kop and a particular Joey Jones banner. Imagine my pleasure at seeing the very same flag being paraded again at the Kop's finale. Before the game, many of the club's greats were paraded: Albert Stubbins, Billy Liddell, Ian Callaghan and Kenny Dalglish, to name a few. However, the biggest cheer was for Nessie Shankly and Jessie Paisley, who were led out arm in arm with Joe Fagan. The Kop sang Shankly to the tune of 'Amazing Grace'. There was a lump in my throat, and the hairs on the back of my neck stood up—a moment I will never forget. Gerry Marsden then led the Kop in the pre-match 'You'll Never Walk Alone', and, again, the supporters did themselves proud.

Then the football commenced, and, as we'd seen time and time again that season, the team let us down. Jeremy Goss scored the last goal in front of the Kop, and Norwich City won 1-0. A fellow Kopite, Gavin Aldridge, and I took our time in leaving the proud old stand and savoured every last moment. Gavin left a flag and I a scarf on the crash barrier where we always stood, and, as our bus pulled away to head south, I took one last look at the Kop. As a regular at Anfield between 1989 and 1996, the Kop was where I had my football education, not only from what was happening on the pitch, but also from those around me. Liverpool supporters sought to be original, fair-minded to their

own and to the opposition and, of course, there was the humour. Where I stood, to the back corner of the Kop, I would often listen to the more senior supporters and, on one occasion, was told how Ronnie Rosenthal reminded one fan of Jackie Balmer of 1940s Liverpool fame. Also there were the less complimentary comments, such as Nicky Tanner being told by one Kopite that he was the worst footballer ever born to a woman—but in far more colourful language. I enjoyed the pre-match beer and banter with friends in the Oakfield and the buzz on the Kop when the team were on song.

The final acts of the 1993/94 campaign were played out against Aston Villa on 7 May, when we witnessed a 2-1 defeat, but most memorable were the half-time celebrations among the Liverpool fans on hearing that Everton were 2-0 down at home to Wimbledon and staring relegation in the face. However, the Blues recovered in the second half and won, much to our dismay! The Liverpool goal at Villa Park that afternoon was scored by Robbie Fowler, who was the silver lining of an otherwise poor season, but at least there was hope for the future.

Unlike many of my peers, I did not go to university, join the army or travel abroad. Liverpool Football Club was my place of learning and adventure, and supporting the Reds allowed me to travel to every corner of the UK and Europe, which I would not have done otherwise. I've met so many people, from all walks of life, along the way, too.

Simon King

COOPERMAN
TO THE RESCUE

Wembley, 13 March 1982, is certainly a day I will never forget—for all the right reasons. But the Liverpool win was especially significant. At that time I was Russ Abbot's personal assistant, and we were both working at London Weekend Television recording Madhouse. As Russ and I are big Liverpool fans and, as ITV was screening the final, the kind souls in the World of Sport office helped us obtain tickets for the match. Like big kids, we were both so excited and had a real crack with all the Liverpool fans around us during the game.

As anyone who remembers the final will recall, Steve Archibald's goal had given Spurs the advantage, and, with five minutes to go and time running out, Russ and I decided to make a move towards the exit as we couldn't see Liverpool getting back in the match. As we stood up, a fanatical Red screamed at Russ, 'Russ, get Cooperman!' Russ looked around and replied, 'Sorry, there's no phone box!' The fan stood to his feet and screamed again, 'Someone find us a phone box, quick!'

We should obviously have had more faith in the Reds that day because as we were walking down the steps towards the exit, we heard an almighty roar, so we rushed back towards our seats to discover that Ronnie Whelan had equalised—extra time was now beckoning. As we re-emerged, the same fan stood before us, with tears in his eyes. He shook our hands, gave us both a big hug and said in total seriousness, 'Thank you Cooperman, thank you!' It was a very touching moment, if slightly surreal! During extra time, another goal from Ronnie Whelan and one from Ian Rush made for a very special conclusion to the day.

Bill Priddin *pictured (left) with Cooperman*

BUGS BUNNY BOXERS

Born and bred in Anfield, just a short walk from the ground, I will never forget the day that our neighbour, Teddy Littlewood, asked if I wanted to go to the game. Teddy had worked at Liverpool as bar manager for quite some time, and, when we arrived at the stadium, he showed me around the place and introduced me to the players. Jan Molby was first up and was lying on a treatment table wearing Bugs Bunny boxer shorts. He was getting a massage from a physio and was very friendly and chatty. He told me not to tell my mum about the boxer shorts. We then moved on to the manager's office where Kenny Dalglish was sat behind his desk. 'I'm just showing my lad around', Teddy explained as I stood looking at the King. I also remember going to the loo and being flanked by Alan Hansen on one side and Jan Molby on the other. I was stuck in the middle and felt honoured to be there.

As a young lad of eight, I was completely star-struck and took the opportunity to get my programme and photos signed by anyone and everyone, and, after a few more home games, the players got to know me and I knew them. I felt like a million dollars. At kick-off, I was given a chipboard stool, which had four rickety legs, and was led to the paddock where I literally squeezed on the end of the row where the stewards would stand and watch the game until the final whistle. This wonderful match day routine lasted until I was 13, when we would nip off just before the final whistle, put our stools away, then go into the players' lounge through the paddock.

During this time, Ian Rush was an ever-present, along with his silver-haired dad, who would occupy the bar at every game. Ray Houghton would come in, and we would watch the final scores coming in on the vidiprinter. The TV was situated at the end of the lounge and the players would hover around to catch the final scores. I also remember the glamour of Gary Ablett's wife, with her dark, permed hair and make-up.

My parents still live in Stanley Park Avenue South, but match days are very different now. Parking permits mean that local children can no longer charge for looking after people's cars, and the players aren't seen in and around the stadium apart from on match days, but I will remember those happy days forever.

Steve Bogg

OUR FOND FAREWELL

It was the last day of standing on the Kop, and the city was at fever pitch. Supporters had been gearing up for weeks before, trying to get their hands on tickets, deciding who they were going with, what songs to sing, what banners or flags to take—all anxious to be there to celebrate and remember the great players and managers who had graced the pitch and played in front of the proud old stand and all those great days and nights, standing side by side with our fellow Liverpool supporters. I chose to go with my school pals. It was a beautiful sunny Saturday, and, as I got dressed in my Liverpool top, I was already singing Reds songs when I walked down to breakfast with my match ticket in hand. I had a laugh with my parents and little sis about how excited I was, then headed off to see my pals and get to the ground really early. There was already a fantastic atmosphere starting to build—the chanting and flag-waving was awesome—but the sight of thousands of Liverpool supporters outside Anfield, bouncing up and down, singing all the classics, is something I will always remember. Queuing up to get into the ground, we even had a jolly with the coppers on horses before we were finally in and making our way to our favourite vantage point to take in one last fling. There were lots of flares being let off, which added to the intensity of the occasion and signalled the start of a ceremony where so many Liverpool legends—and the sight of Bill Shankly's wife—prompted a huge roar of approval and appreciation. It seemed unnatural that Liverpool lost the game 1-0, Norwich's Jeremy Goss ironically scoring at the very end. However, it seemed that the Reds fans weren't too concerned about the result. We were all there to celebrate the Kop that afternoon. I think it would be fair to say that everybody present, in all parts of the ground, was filled with a mixture of emotions, mainly happy ones, remembering all the wonderful times spent rejoicing together.

Stephen Ainscough

REVISING MY PLANS

I was never a brilliant student at school. My revision master plan usually consisted of last-minute studying, often the night before a final exam itself, and a sudden interest in all matters religious in the vain hope that the universe would generously devise a way to get me the desired grade. But as I was to discover in 2005, Liverpool Football Club made me abandon even those desperate methods.

I was in my second year of college, and it was the night before an important history exam. More importantly, it was also the night of the second leg of the Liverpool vs Juventus Champions League quarter-final. Carrying a 2-1 advantage from the previous week's win at Anfield, I was on tenterhooks and wore a spaced-out, 'mind elsewhere' look all day—the look I get whenever attempts are made to discuss non-football-type things with me when there are more pressing matters at hand. So, insisting to my mother that I would have to revise all night in my self-designated study room (which coincidentally had a television), I settled down to watch the match with my textbook opened in front of me, at least trying to make the scene look partially authentic in case of a sudden parental check. Everyone at home slept while I made myself comfortable in front of the television screen.

Every free-kick, every corner, every minute of every second caused me to question why I put myself through this torture every game and WHY it never seemed to get any easier. Anyway, such thoughts were fleeting as I was brought back to the present by one of many close calls. But then, in that state of mind, even an intercepted Liverpool throw-in set me off into a panic ahead of a 'certain goal' for the opposition. I survived, though, and so did my club. Thankfully the Reds were through to the semi-finals. With happiness and immense relief racing through my veins, I thought

I should at least put in an hour or two flicking through my history book after the match, but football was all that I could think about, so I gave up and went to bed.

The next day, in the examination room, I was faced with a very unfamiliar-looking question paper that I wondered what the hell I was supposed to do with. Anyone looking at me would have mistaken the expression on my face as one of joy or confidence about the exam ahead, but unknown to them, I was of course thinking about the match the night before because I didn't have a clue what to write. I was completely unprepared. I jotted down a few half-hearted things on my piece of paper, whatever I could summon from my sieve-like brain, but as the results were to show a month later, it wasn't enough. I failed, and I would have to wait another year to make amends. I admit that I did panic momentarily, but I also realised that exams would come and go. Champions League campaigns like that come along just once in a blue moon. I may have failed history, but history DEFINITELY didn't fail me.

Shreya Chakravertty

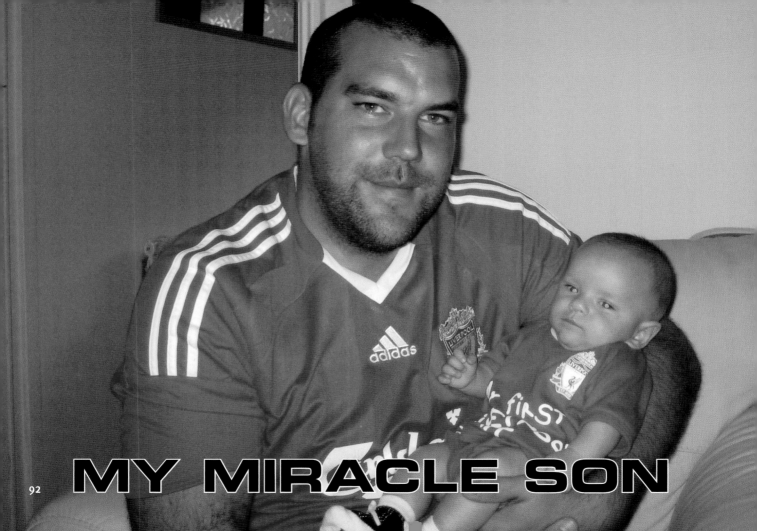

MY MIRACLE SON

I'm a huge Liverpool fan, and, although I live in south Wales, I try my hardest to get up to see the team as much as I can. However, this has happened less since the birth of my son, which is where my story begins. Max was born on 10 March 2009, but, as he was three months premature, he weighed just one pound and 15 ounces—a real fighter who should not really be here today. I had been filled with a mixture of fear as well as happiness all day but, eventually, I had to leave my wife and new son in hospital and return home for the night. As it was also the same day as Liverpool's Champions League match against Real Madrid, the game was perfectly timed to take my mind off events. But before I left my new son that evening, I sang Max some Liverpool songs, including 'The Fields of Anfield Road' and 'Torres, Torres', to keep him strong through the night. And, when Liverpool ran out 4-0 winners, I knew it had been my son's arrival that had been the deciding factor and that had brought that little bit of luck that was needed.

After that, I continued singing Liverpool songs to Max, as they genuinely seemed to be calming to him, and I became more and more convinced that his arrival was a lucky charm for the Reds, especially when we beat Manchester United 4-1 in our next match. I started to think that 2009 was going to be our year at last—the two biggest games of the season and we'd smashed them. Then the Reds beat Aston Villa 5-0 and Blackburn 1-0, a sequence of events that was surely all down to my miracle son. The positive string of results was also keeping my belief strong, too. It seemed that his arrival at that point was meant to be, it was helping Liverpool and, in return, Liverpool's victories kept me believing that Max would be ok.

Inevitably, the winning run came to an end, and, although he still can't talk, Max always responds to the Liverpool renditions, and he clearly enjoys it when his great grandad, Jack Thomson from Maghull, sings 'You'll Never Walk Alone' to him. My wife, Laura, and I both want Max to be a Liverpool fan just like us, and, when he is big enough, we will take him to his first game where no doubt his knack of bringing good fortune will come flooding back. Our family also wants him to be a mascot one day—an event that will surely coincide with Liverpool winning the Premier League!

Mathew Pullen

THE BOY WHO LIVED THE DREAM

How many Liverpool fans remember the date 26 May 1999 with much affection? Not many, I guess, as this was the day a team just down the M62 scored two late goals to win a European Cup final. But for me this was a truly memorable day. You see, I had an interview at Liverpool Football Club that day, and, at eight minutes past six in the evening—I remember it well—I received a phone call to inform me that I was the newly appointed manager of the, as yet unnamed, education centre to be built next to the LFC Museum at Anfield Stadium. The same famous Anfield Stadium I first visited when I was just seven years old to see my first ever Liverpool game with my dad.

Born into a family of Liverpool FC fanatics, could there be a better job for me? I don't think so. I started my job on 1 September, and 'Little Bamber' Brian Hall was my new boss. I had stood on the terraces at Wembley in 1974 and watched him on the pitch as we hammered Newcastle 3-0, and now I was sitting next to him, discussing my new role at the club. How many times did I pinch myself to remind me this was not just a dream? Brian introduced me to a clever man who he said could think up a fab name for the new education centre. He came up with 'Reduc@te', a mix, he said, of 'red' and 'educate'. I loved it and went with it. He later sent a bill for £20,000 for the use of the name. He really was a clever man.

Brian organised a former players' party in Reduc@te at Christmas, and lots of ex-Reds came, as you would expect. I met my boyhood hero Ian Callaghan and had my photo taken with him. Roger Hunt was there with Ian St John and Ron Yeats and Kevin Keegan, too. That was my best Christmas since I woke up and found a Johnny Seven under the tree. I even saw Sammy Lee, who I had last met on a football pitch in 1973 in the Liverpool Echo Cup final. He was captain of SFX, and I was captain of West Derby Comp. We won 2-0, and I reminded Sammy that this was one medal he didn't win in his great career. How I laughed, alone. We are back on speaking terms now, though.

The club gave me a minibus to transport the children, and we went to Melwood in it, all excited to have a photo with a player. Would it be Robbie Fowler or Michael Owen, perhaps? We got there late, and Mr Houllier said an up-and-coming player would have to suffice as the first team was already out training. His name was Steven Gerrard. Beggars can't be choosers, I suppose. Reduc@te opened officially in July 2000. Lucy Meacock came along, and we were on the telly! She was the first of a string of TV people who have visited over the years. Sunita from Corrie came with the barmaid from the Rovers Return and so did Denzel

from Only Fools and Horses. We had evicted Big Brother contestants by the dozens. 'Bubble' paid us a visit, and I told him a joke. He laughed, fit to burst. We even had royalty. The Crown Prince of Brunei came along and asked me why I had decorated Reduc@te with flags of Dubai. I always read my emails properly after that. And players! Sami Hyypia came in with his family in 2002. The man from the Public Relations Department, Vin O'Brien, knew I was a big cricket fan and asked me to explain the rules of cricket to Sami as they don't play it in Finland. Sami listened, said nothing, and never came back. Michael Owen came in to do a Noel Edmunds Christmas Special with some children, which went out after the Queen's speech on Christmas Day. I did all I could to be in the background of every shot but never made it past the cutting room floor. Milan Baros came in to launch our website 'Hola' in 2004, and Emile Heskey came in once, so I explained how we had a Reduc@te game called 'Heskey's Hat-trick'. He asked if it was named after him. Goalkeeper Chris Kirkland was an LFC Reading Star, and he came in to talk about his favourite book and sign autographs for some children. I gave him a big, thick marker pen, and he dropped it on the floor.

Liverpool Football Club has been good to me. They have taken me to cup finals all over the place. The carnivals in Cardiff, the joy of Germany, the inspiration that was Istanbul and the grief of Greece. They let me sit behind the goal and take photos of games. The glamour job of a photographer is not so glamorous when the cold has frozen your fingers to the bone, the rain is lashing down and you are soaked to the skin and dripping like a gutter. I have even sat in the Directors' Box and have been on the pitch at half-time to receive an award. I looked up to the seat in the Main Stand where my dad used to sit all those years ago and wished so much he could have shared that moment. One year, on a players' visit to meet children at Alder Hey Hospital in West Derby, I even drove 14 of the players in the Reduc@te minibus back to Melwood as the proper bus hadn't turned up. I was shaking like a leaf! Carra and Stevie G were in the back and Harry Kewell and John Arne Riise sat next to me in the front and barked directions on the mile-long journey.

I have lived in West Derby all my life but thanked an Australian and a Norwegian for guiding me back to base. Star-struck I surely was! I have been to the most fabulous staff Christmas parties at Anfield and wore fancy dress to most of them. I won a prize as Diana Ross. It was a supreme effort. I sweated inside a snowman outfit one year and again the next as a spaceman. I had my photo taken with John Bishop, who did a turn at one of our parties once. He told me he was just starting out in stand-up. He was okay, but I thought, 'Don't give up your day job.' I have loved my 11 years working at the best football club in the world. I have met so many special people, enjoyed so many great events and watched so many exhilarating matches. Istanbul stands out, and I am privileged to say that 'I was there', as the picture shows. I made it there and back, even though only half of my glasses did.

U.S. President Truman memorably said, 'If you can't stand the heat, get out of the kitchen', and sadly that is what I have had to do. Reduc@te closed in May 2010 to become a kitchen for the sumptuous new 'Boot Room' restaurant. But a new, bigger and brighter Learning Centre has been built so that thousands more fantastic kids from the city and beyond can learn enthusiastically, using the inspirational environment of Liverpool Football Club to aid their progress. Will I be there with them? I hope so, and my defrosted fingers are well and truly crossed. But they do say all good things come to an end. So, just in case I am not, thank you to all the wonderful staff who have helped me over the years to make Reduc@te a 'way of life', and thank you, Liverpool Football Club, for all you have done for me. How lucky have I been, the boy who lived the dream!

Keith White

A ROLLERCOASTER OF A DAY OUT

When we reached the FA Cup final in 2006, I decided to treat my wife and get her a ticket for the big game as a birthday present, which I secured through a handy contact I had at the FA. I then looked at the travel options from our home in Sheffield to Cardiff. Train prices were so expensive that I even turned to thoughts of treating us to a chauffeur-driven car; however, having been priced out of a limousine, I enquired about a Mercedes or a BMW. A couple of phone calls later, and I had been quoted £180 there and back, door to door, which was only marginally more than by rail, so I was happy to agree and made arrangements.

Fast forward to the big match day. The excitement was really building. I had gotten a babysitter for our three young children sorted, and we were confidently looking forward to watching Liverpool win another trophy. As the agreed pick-up time approached, I paced up and down the street, excitedly looking for the driver to turn up so that we could be on our way, but pick-up time came and went and I started to get more than a bit nervous. It was now already past 11.30am, and there were more than 200 miles to travel if we were to make the 3pm kick-off. When I anxiously phoned the car company to enquire where on Earth the driver was, I was given the gob-smacking news that, according to their records, there was no booking at all. Despite lots of arguing and disagreements, there was no alternative than to jump into my trusty old Mondeo and set off at a great rate of knots—not always adhering to the limit, I have to admit!

So, although we were at least en route and heading rapidly westward, there was still another major hurdle to jump over, namely we still didn't have our match tickets because my contact didn't trust the postal service following the robbery of a post van. Some match tickets were in the haul, so ours would be handed to us by a lady at the ground. I was constantly receiving calls from my contact on the way, asking if I was there yet. 'Almost!' I kept telling her, but in reality we were still over 120 miles away. As we got closer to Cardiff, I phoned and explained the situation to her, but she told me that she'd waited as long as she could and was going into the stadium and she would pass our tickets onto another of her colleagues. We finally made it into Cardiff 10 minutes before kick-off, so I left my wife to park the car while I ran to the ground to grab the tickets. As the stadium came into view, I tried to phone her, but, to my utter dismay, I couldn't get a reception on my mobile. Then, when it finally kicked back in, she obviously didn't hear her phone ringing as it diverted to her answer phone. It was a complete nightmare. Thankfully, with my nerves in tatters, we eventually made contact, and, finally, we exchanged tickets and I went off to find my wife. She parked, then we both legged it back to the ground.

As we reached the gate, a fellow Liverpool fan offered me £400 for my ticket, but there was no way I could contemplate missing the game after the grief we'd had getting that far. By 3.06pm, we had finally taken our seats and could breath a huge sigh of relief. We could relax and enjoy a comfortable win for the Reds. How wrong I was!

As you will all recall, within 20 minutes of taking our seats, the Reds were 2-0 down. We were the European Champions, that shouldn't be happening, surely? Thankfully we pulled it back to 2-2, but a mistake from the previously unflappable Pepe Reina meant that Liverpool were heading towards injury time 3-2 down. As the final whistle approached, I thought to myself: 'Should we just make an early exit, avoid some of the traffic and, hopefully, at least have an easier journey home?' I then remembered the spirit of Istanbul just 12 months earlier and decided that idea was best kept quiet. Instead I turned my attention back to the game. The fourth official held up

his board, which indicated four minutes of injury time. I then gazed back towards the pitch and watched in amazement as Captain Fantastic smashed the ball into the net and saved the day...again! OH MY GOD...I WENT MENTAL!

I don't know what the players were feeling as the game moved into extra time, but, personally, I had never been so physically or mentally drained during a football match. Then, as penalties drew ever closer, I turned to the fan next to me and told him how we would win the game on spot-kicks. Thankfully I was proven right, and there was loads of shouting, dancing, cheering and hugging everywhere I looked. We had won the FA Cup again, the world's most famous cup competition, and every Liverpool fan was jumping with joy. As the team were presented with the wonderful trophy, and during the subsequent laps of honour, the atmosphere was amazing. Then, once the players headed off back to the dressing room for more celebrations, we decided to head back towards the car, stopping off for a quick sing-song with Johnny Vegas and a few hundred fans outside a pub.

I don't remember much about the journey home, but I do know that I'd lost my voice from all the singing and shouting, and I was completely exhausted—but what a day! It was a rollercoaster of a day that I will never forget. One filled with such mixed emotion: anticipation, worry, anger, relief, pain and, finally, joy! But, then again, that is what happens when you are part of the family that is Liverpool Football Club.

Gary Armstrong

BILL'S NEW RIGHT-HAND GIRL

In early 1963, there was an advert in the Liverpool Echo, which read: 'Liverpool Football Club— Junior Secretary required', so I applied for an interview. I lived in Finchley Road at the time, a five-minute walk from the ground, so on the day of the interview, I headed around to Anfield Road. I must have been the first to be interviewed because there was no one else there. I was called into the office, and there was Bill Shankly and another man. He turned out to be the manager of The Stadium in Liverpool, which was a well-known boxing and wrestling venue. He was a friend of Bill's, and as the Liverpool manager had never interviewed a secretary before, he had come to help out.

The interview didn't last long, and Bill and I hit it off from the start. At the end, Bill said, 'Susan, you've got the job. Can you start on Monday?' To which his friend said, 'No, Bill, you can't do that; there are other people waiting to be interviewed.' Bill replied, 'Oh yes', then added, 'Susan, come with me', and led me to the room next door. A short time later, Bill came back and, in his broad Scottish accent, said, 'Right, Susan, now you've definitely got the job! Can you start a week on Monday?' I said that I could, and he replied, 'Good, let's have a drink. Will you have a whiskey?' I floated home that day, but it wasn't anything to do with the drink. I was going to be working at Liverpool Football Club and for Bill Shankly!

At the time, I worked as a shorthand typist for John Taylor's, a ship's chandler's company near the Pier Head. The LFC interview was on a Friday, and, although I didn't normally work on a Saturday, I realised that I would have to go in to give a week's notice. Looking back, I was young

and naïve, and it didn't even occur to me that the people at John Taylor's might be annoyed at having to find a replacement at such short notice. So I went in the following morning, and, when I told them I was going to be working for Bill Shankly, they were so pleased for me. I had worked for Taylor's since leaving school at 15, and they were like an extended family, so I'd sometimes pop back on occasions to chat about the club, and they would send out for cakes. Such was the strength of feeling for LFC.

On my first day, Bill showed me around, and it was April Fool's day, which he never forgot. Bill had a tiny office under the Main Stand, directly below the Directors' Box. My office was next to his, but it was bigger than his. When he had a meeting, he'd say, 'Susan, go and have a cup of tea', so that he could use my office! In the beginning, he didn't know what to do with me as he had been used to doing his own letters and had a small, portable typewriter, which he used to take with him on the coach when travelling to away games. Bill liked replying to fans' questions regarding why he'd played a certain player or why he'd selected a particular formation. Initially I only had a couple of letters to do in the mornings because, at about 9.30am, he would change into his tracksuit and set off to the training ground at Melwood, returning at about midday. The 'B Stand' cafeteria was used as the canteen, and all the players and staff would go there for lunch. Every Monday there was rice pudding on the menu, and Bill would nudge whoever was nearest then say, 'Come on Susan, have some of that rice pudding, it'll put hairs on your chest!' The thought of saying that to an 18-year-old girl would send him into fits of laughter. When I was at school, we were encouraged to consider other languages and have a pen pal, so I wrote to a boy in East Germany, which was under Communist control at that time, and when I mentioned him to Bill, he once wrote, 'Well, at least he's the right colour. Red!'

After a short while, I would wander into the main office to see if there was anything I could help them with. In fact, I spent so much time in the main office that I eventually moved in. It was a small office with a couple of phones and a small switchboard, and on one wall there was a small window which was known as the 'ticket window'. There was also a large safe, which was quite flashy and took up a lot of room, but the inside was tiny. When we'd won the FA Cup, we had to decide whether to put the trophy in the safe or the tickets for the European Cup (they could burn) but there wasn't room for both! There were only two people in the main office, Tom Bush and Bill Barlow, and I offered to help, they were only too happy to give me some work. They pointed to a couple of boxes, and I opened them to find they were full of letters and postal orders from fans who wanted old programmes and the like.

You have to remember that this was the early '60s and 'merchandising' was a thing of the future. The club didn't sell anything, and most of the red and white striped Liverpool scarves were probably knitted by mums and wives! The Supporters' Club may have sold a handful, but I think Liverpool's first taste of 'enterprise' was when we moved a caravan into the car park, and someone sold tickets for guessing the time of the first goal. Later on, the caravan grew into a Portakabin. On a match day at half-time, I would hop down to the office to answer the endless phone calls from fans wanting to know the latest score, because if the match wasn't on the radio it was their only way of finding out. Equally, if there were a goal during the match, fans would hear the roar and ring up to find out who had scored. The phone would be red hot, literally!

On the day I passed my driving test, there was very heavy snow, and there was an international match that evening. During the game, the snow changed to sleet, and the visibility was so bad that the match was abandoned. It must have been the first time it had happened because there wasn't a plan for refunds. I ended up standing at the 'ticket window' until almost midnight writing down the names and addresses of fans so they could get a refund—if only we had today's technology In the end, the Chief Constable said I should go home, and, because of the horrendous weather conditions, he instructed a couple of his boys to take me home in a squad car.

When we won the FA Cup in '65, we went to the Liverpool Town Hall, and the roads were a sea of bodies. It was a fantastic sight! When the coach finally got to the Town Hall, there were two ows of police either side of the entrance. They had linked arms and were trying hard to keep the crowds back to allow the team into the Town Hall. The players got in ok, but I was the only female and was struggling to keep up in my heels so, before I knew it, the police had picked me up and was being passed down the line like 'pass the parcel'—my feet never touched the ground! It was a great day.

The Boot Room was a gathering place where the training staff could sit and have a 'chunner' as well as watch horse racing on the television. One day, I went down there to have a word with Bob Paisley, and he said, 'Sit down and have a glass of Guinness.' I was very slim, and the guys were always trying to feed me up, but every so often I'd go down to the Boot Room just to sit and natter with Bob and Joe, who were always so friendly.

Liverpool had never been a 'flash' club, and when I look back, the facilities were quite poor but nobody thought anything about it. The supporters were used to the Kop, they were used to standing in rows with small barriers between them, and the seats in the stand were simply hard wooden benches, while they liked standing in the Paddock. They thought they were up-market in the Paddock because they were standing alongside the action. When we had Kemlyn Road built we thought we'd really arrived. It was a cantilever affair, and, instead of standing in the rain, fans could sit in the rain instead.

On a match day, it could get very manic, with people turning up to see if they'd been left tickets, players arriving wanting something or another, even the odd celeb. There was a real buzz about the place, exciting times indeed, but you had to be prepared to do anything. Talking of celebs, when I worked at John Taylor's, I would get the bus into town, and Cilla Black used to get on the same bus, if she made it. She lived on Scotland Road and worked off Dale Street and she was often late. On a morning, I would see her trying to put her coat on while wrestling with a piece of toast! We weren't friends, but I knew her because we both went to the Cavern at lunchtime. It was before all the groups became famous, so it was normal to see the Beatles, Gerry and the Pacemakers, Rory Storm, the Big 3 and most of the Manchester groups. Cilla sometimes helped in the cloakroom and, on occasions, would go on stage, but the only thing I can remember her singing was 'Fever'. At lunchtime, you could choose between tomato or oxtail soup, take it or leave it!

In 1967, I met a Royal Marine Commando from Aintree, and in 1968, we were married. The team was due to come to the wedding, but unfortunately they drew in an FA Cup match on the Saturday and had the replay on the Monday evening so couldn't come. The only player able to attend was Geoff Twentyman, and there was even a picture in the paper of me in my wedding dress with the headline 'Smiling through her disappointment'. It made my husband Brian laugh, but he still maintains that they failed to show up because I married him!

We live in Surrey now and come home to 'the Pool' a couple of times a year, and we are always thrilled to see that today's Liverpudlians are still as friendly, chatty and vibrant as ever. From Singapore to Canada (and all points in between), I have sat with a radio pressed to my ear in an attempt to listen to the match, and all I can say is, thank goodness for the internet and LFCTV! I was very lucky to have grown up in Liverpool during that wonderful era and to have worked at the club was absolutely fantastic! My heart will always be with Liverpool Football Club and with the city—I will also always remember the wonderful personalities I worked alongside.

Susan Mowll (nee Hamblet)

ROME '77

Wednesday evening, 5 o'clock the 25th of May
And Rome's a taken city, well, at least for the day

The Spanish steps and the Coliseum, what do they recall?
Not Romans, nor Gladiators, but a match, a game of football

Kevin Keegan and Joey Jones songs ring out from every arch
Paisley's giant Red Army has started its glorious march

Terry Mac and Tommy Smith put the Reds ahead
Then Kevin and Phil Neal put the Gladbachs to bed

Liverpool 3 München 1, in the year of '77
All our dreams came true, and so did Shanks' who was watching from heaven.

David Corcoran
Written somewhere in northern Italy on a train bound for home,
26 May 1977

OU EST LE STADE?

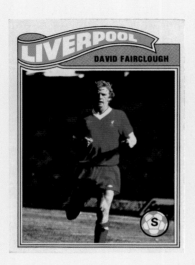

What made me do it? I lived in Birmingham. I had no ticket. It was probably because Liverpool hadn't been this far in the European Cup since 1965 (before my time), and the fans didn't know when it would happen again. Those were the days when only League Champions took part in the European Cup. For me, it was a whole new experience, as I had only been supporting the Reds seriously since 1969. So off I went. Train from Birmingham to Liverpool Lime Street. Bus to Anfield. I got there with nearly an hour to spare. I could hear the crowd singing, could see the lights, could almost feel the ground beneath me shaking. But the gates were locked. Bolted. I was shut out. Half of me was deliriously happy to feel the atmosphere, half bitterly disappointed to be shut out, and I cursed myself for my stupid whim. I mooched around outside the ground for what seemed like ages. Then, as I stood in the car park, behind the Main Stand, I heard a loud yelling behind me. I turned round. There was a crowd of young men haring towards me. 'Uh oh!' I thought, this was a hooligan-rife era, after all. 'Trouble! What do I do now?' But they passed me and headed for a pair of locked gates. They shook, they heaved, they pulled. The gates cracked open, and they all disappeared inside. I looked around. Nobody was watching me. Nobody had emerged to see what had happened. Guiltily and furtively, I stepped through, then climbed various sets of steps, eventually coming out onto a crowded sliver, a small V of terracing that, in those days, adjoined the Main Stand. I could see the pitch in front of me, I could see the Kop to the right and I could see and hear thousands of excited, singing supporters. Soon the match started. Liverpool were attacking the Anfield Road end in the first half, so from where I was standing, I couldn't really see the goal that cancelled the first-leg deficit. In fact, I don't remember much at all of the first half, but I do remember the constant singing, the atmosphere of hope and 'victory in the air'. If we won this, we'd be through to the semi-finals for only the second time in our history. Thus it was, early in the second period, that I also missed the Saint-Étienne equaliser that put them 2-1 up in the tie on aggregate. It was deadly serious all of a sudden. The away goal meant Liverpool needed to score twice to get through now. I don't remember Ray Kennedy's goal, except that it was a cause for renewed singing, hope and expectation. But even now, 33 years on, I can picture the scene 10 minutes from time when carrot-haired 'Super Sub' David Fairclough ran onto a through ball. I have a mental image of our most famous redhead dribbling at speed for what seemed to be a third of the pitch to calmly slot the ball home in front of the Kop and make the score 3-1. And we were through. I decided to leave promptly at the final whistle. If I hurried, I could catch a bus to my parents' house in Thornton and catch the match highlights on TV—no live European games in those days except the European Cup final. But the night wasn't quite over. Before I got to Walton Breck Road to catch sight of a coach-load of disappointed Saint-Étienne supporters pick its way through traffic, I walked down the darkened terrace streets that surround Anfield. And coming the other way was a little man in a brown raincoat and wearing a trilby hat. Around his neck was one of those serious-looking 1950s cameras, and, as he approached me, he said something about 'West Ham'. I thought, 'What? Who is this idiot?' He repeated himself, and suddenly I realised he was French, and he was asking, '*Ou est le stade?*' ('Where is the stadium?'). I waved my arm in the direction of Anfield and added in my finest Franglaise, 'La, monsieur. La. We won!' He simply smiled and walked off towards the ground, to do what, I'm not quite sure. I think he'd got lost and missed the match completely, but I hadn't. I was there, I was at Anfield for the best match I've ever been to. Truly a night to remember.

Chris Rigby

IT'S A FAMILY THING

In May 1945, my great-grandmother received a telegram from Major Mae Kay, notifying her that her son had been killed in action. The local newspaper reported, 'Liverpool player Private Stanley Sheldrake, aged 19, from 66 Venmore Street, Anfield, L4, was accidentally killed in Germany. Stan [pictured left], an inside-forward, who was an old boy of Breckfield Council School, where he captained the football team, later playing for Liverpool Boys' FC, where he won several medals. Only one week before his death he had signed on for post-war football with Liverpool Football Cub.' The tragic death of Stan linked our family even closer to the club, but Liverpool FC had already been a big part of the family for many years, with my great-grandfather, Stan's father, signing on a weekly basis from about 1910. All the family went to watch in those days; football was an integral part of the Scouse community, a shared collective passion at the end of a hard working week.

My dad, Bill Thompson Jr, and his sister, Hilary, described the exciting times of growing up in the shadow of the Kop. As a boy, my dad remembers regularly going with his dad in the '50s and weaving his way through supporters' legs, and recalls, after a heavy snowfall the day before a game, the club asking local boys to clear snow from the steps of Anfield so that the match could go ahead in return for free admission. Like many from that generation, matches that stick out in his mind are the 1965 Cup final and the home games with Inter Milan and Saint-Étienne, especially with the atmosphere generated, with European matches being new territory. Shankly's reign turned Liverpool into a unique club and created fearless fans who believed they could beat anyone in any circumstances, creating an unrivalled atmosphere.

As fans, we always had a good understanding of the game and respect for other teams' good football. We were the original fans, creating unique chants, banners, signs and flags. Other teams copied us, in an attempt to emulate our success, but we can profess never to have been manufactured. Through the success and spreading support, my dad remembers the crowds trying to get into Anfield—queues five and six deep stretching around Stanley Park to get FA Cup final tickets. Dad used to pay at the gate for each game. He bought his first season ticket for the Kop when he was 14 and remembers swaying on the Kop, singing, including Beatles songs, and the contagious ambition, hard work and aura of the great Shankly and Paisley and our players, which turned Liverpool into the most successful club in the land. It was the beginning of an illustrious alliance between the club, players, managers and fans, who all played a key role in transforming the club.

During this era, my nan would regularly chat to Liverpool managers and players in the local shops, where they would buy fruit and such for the team. One particular day, Bob Paisley greeted nan, asking how she was. Nan mentioned she had a problem with her neck, so he said, 'Elsie, come down to the club, and we'll sort it out for you.' Can you imagine that happening now? They were respected local heroes but remained ordinary, down-to-earth people who lived close to the ground. Our family joined the original Liverpool Supporters' Club, travelling to away matches and attending events and weekly meetings; the club was at the very heart of the community.

Dad would play footy every night with his mates on Stanley Park, and apprentice players, who were renting accommodations around the ground, including Kenny Dalglish, would join in. As Liverpool grew in stature, the ground became a hive of activity, and it was an exciting place to live. 113

66 Venmore Street, Anfield, was our family home from 1942; the family had lived further up the same road but moved after being bombed in the blitz, and my grandparents remained there till the late 1990s when they died. The house was also the heart of our family's long-standing support of LFC for decades.

I was a European Cup baby, due on the week of Liverpool's first final in 1977, but my first ever Reds memory came at age three when my grandad took my dear cousin, Paul, and me to the Supporters' Club Christmas party. Nan's love for her treasured Liverpool was infectious, and she adored that, on match days, all her children, grandchildren and extended family would arrive to celebrate their devotion to Liverpool. It was like a family party every weekend, with my nan preparing food for any family or friends that called in on their way back from the game. After the match, my nan would stand on her doorstep asking the score (although she already knew it), enjoying the banter with the fans walking past her house. When we were too small to go to the game, we played football in the back yard, listening for the roars from the ground, and then rushed inside to listen to the radio to see who had scored, you could feel the excitement even from outside the ground. I was desperate to go to my first game, eventually getting that opportunity at six. I was unbearably excited and remember climbing the steps in the Main Stand and seeing the pitch for the first time—I was mesmerised by how beautiful it looked—and then watching the swaying of the Kop and listening to the songs. I loved it.

Luckily, we used to get spare tickets every week, so I became a regular. My nan would dress me in an old Liverpool silk scarf and give me a bar of chocolate. Then I used to head off with my grandad and Paul to the Main Stand, with the rest of the family going in the Kop. We'd then all meet up again afterwards back at number 66 for tea and a post-match chat. My cousins, Paul, Daniel and Graham, and I spent hours learning all the songs in the front room of Venmore with my nan playing on the piano, and on the wall was an embroidered picture of the LFC badge. My grandad continued to go to the match each week until he was 90. When I was a child, LFC was my obsession, and, examining my old primary school books, it proves that the football club was all that I wrote about and that Rush was my hero. There wasn't much memorabilia around in those days, but my nan would get us what there was, and always got us a Liverpool FC Christmas card and calendar.

As far as my obsession is concerned, nothing much has changed now that I'm an adult. I still love my club to bits; I never miss a game, whether it is a friendly, a qualifier or a Carling Cup fixture at a half-filled Anfield in freezing conditions. I never tire of going to Anfield and standing to sing our amazing songs. It's my favourite place in the world. Dusty boxes containing hundreds of programmes of unbelievable games we have attended over the years are housed in our loft. I remember the homecoming after the 1989 FA Cup final, as we stood on Breck Road, watching the players pass with the trophy and seeing my nan fill up with tears. She stood there with immense pride as Liverpool passed, but it was also tinged with great sadness as we had lost 96 of our fellow supporters at Hillsborough five weeks earlier, which affected everyone across the city so deeply. As a Liverpool supporter from an early age, I'd learnt how important solidarity is through the bad times as well as the good, and I remember the time when I was 11, when Liverpool became a shrine, where we were all compelled to join each other queuing up around Anfield to lay flowers in the goal to show our respect and that we were one big family. In the '90s, unusually, there were several years that we did not win a trophy. Shanks and Paisley had set the bar of expectation high, but Liverpool supporters are the most committed in the land, and we stuck in there. Support is for life, not just for the good times.

Dad had always told me about his favourite games of the past, but, in 2004/05, under Rafa Benitez, we had a great run in the European Cup and met Chelsea in the semis, playing at home in the second leg. This was my Saint-Étienne moment, and we were so excited that we got to the ground hours before kick-off to discover that most other fans had done the same! The atmosphere was like nothing I had experienced before. It was my best ever game at Anfield, and we drove home after the win, beeping the horn with a big flag sticking out of the sunroof. Unless you are part of this great establishment, it is hard to understand, but it means the world, it runs through the very

core of the family. The final, as if you don't know, was in Istanbul and was the best day of my life. Dad and I travelled to Turkey for the day, and I think this game is the perfect portrayal of a Liverpool supporter's greatest qualities. LFC fans are the most resourceful in the world and had used every way possible to get over to Turkey and get hold of a ticket. Most of the stadium was covered in red, and the sight was absolutely amazing. During the game, we experienced the lows of football, but solidly stood firmly together, supporting and motivating the team against adversity. Most important of all was our undying belief as the 12th man. We generated our unique atmosphere with our great songs and banners and were instrumental in helping turn the game around and winning the cup for the fifth time—for keeps. The Ataturk is my second favourite place in the world—I didn't want to leave, I was so happy. We made it back for the homecoming and had our flag out of the taxi window all the way home from the airport.

Just like my nan, I well up with pride when I think of those two games; they meant so much to me. Shankly was right when he said football is more important than life and death. Most people can't comprehend that magnitude, but I believe being a Liverpool supporter is my best quality, and I am proud to translate these values and experiences I have learnt as a supporter into my life. Liverpool is the most important constitution in the world. Not a minute goes by without LFC being at the forefront of my mind, and, as a family, we have shared the highs and lows and have had a great time. There was only ever one colour in our house—red. So, 100 years on, and just like our predecessors, we still carry out the traditions each week. However, even though 66 Venmore Street survived the blitz, the house was unfortunately knocked down in 2009, a victim of the club's worldwide success. So it had started to kill parts of the community that had made it, but we will always bear the legacy of the Liverbird upon our chest. That will last forever. It's a family thing.

Elizabeth Thompson *in loving memory of Stan Sheldrake, Bill Thompson (Gang), Elsie Thompson and Paul McDonough Y.N.W.A*

10 INSIDE LEFT

LIVERPOOL
"THE REDS"
Anfield Road

OUR FAMILY ANTHEM

My family are die-hard Liverpool supporters, hailing from Dublin's fair city, but none were more passionate than my uncle, Peter Keegan. In the '70s, he was renowned for ringing his wife from Liverpool on payday and informing her that he'd gone over to see the match. God love Aunt Mary, she was a saint. It will be no surprise, then, that Uncle Peter raised his sons to be footballers, as well as passionate Liverpool supporters. They went to games together whenever they could, and, when they couldn't worship at Anfield in person, they cheered from their local pub over a few pints. Kim, his daughter, is a passionate

Red, too. Unfortunately, several years ago, Uncle Peter was diagnosed with terminal cancer, and his eldest son, Paul, who was a professional footballer by that stage, came home to help out. Despite his failing health, Peter never missed a match. When he eventually passed away, his sons buried him in his favourite jersey with his original 1970s Liverpool scarf around his neck—threadbare, not a tassel left on it, but much cherished. His coffin was escorted out of the church to 'You'll Never Walk Alone', what else, but now that song isn't just an anthem to the team we all support, but it is also a salute and reminding nod towards Peter for his passion and unwavering support of the team he loved. Like it is for countless loyal Liverpool households, the song is also a family anthem, and, whenever we hear it, we sing loudly and joyfully and remember.

Deborah Doran

MISSING PERSON

I was a 16-year-old schoolboy and had never been anywhere in my life, apart from different area's in Liverpool and the zoo on a school trip. One Friday night in 1977, on the spur of the moment and completely unannounced, I decided to set off on the Liverpool trip of a lifetime.

My beloved Reds were due to be in Rome to fight for the European Cup. The magnitude of the match was too much for me to cope with—I just had to be there!

So, with just £3 in my pocket, no real idea where I was going and without a passport, I managed to hitch down to London aboard a Reliant Robin, then on to Dover by train, where I caught a ferry over to Calais and another train to Paris—without anyone even asking to check a ticket! Which was handy, because I didn't have one. Unfortunately for me, that's as near as I got to Rome. I was stranded in the wrong country, but I was at least on the continent and was eventually happy in the knowledge Liverpool had won the European Cup.

After eating bread that had been left for pigeons in a Paris park for a couple of days, I decided it was time to visit the British Consul and attempt to get home. Armed with a fabricated story about how I had ended up in the French capital alone, I was told that if somebody back in England agreed to stump up £76, they could provide me with a travel warrant to get me back home.

Unfortunately, knowing that a call home to my parents, who had reported me as a missing person by that stage, was out of the question, I decided to try and get back home the same way as I'd got to Paris in the first place...and it almost worked!

I did manage to get all the way back to Calais, and I did manage to climb over a very big wall and walk back onto a ferry that, I hoped, was heading towards the White Cliffs of Dover, but, just as I thought I'd slipped passed customs, my collar was felt. But then, after the ships Captain had promised that he wouldn't press charges, the police confirmed I was a missing person, and, because I was still a minor and they couldn't just let me go, I was escorted across the Channel and my parents where informed.

Back in Blighty, a travel warrant from Dover to Liverpool was arranged, and, 34 years later, I'm still grounded! The really funny thing about this story is that when I got home and emptied my pockets, I still had the £3 that I'd set off with!

I'm not proud of the worry and anguish that I'd put my parent's through but proud that I am able to tell a story about my love affair with Liverpool FC and the lengths I went to attempting to follow the Reds!

Paul Shinner *pictured with a ticket for the game he missed*

Contributors

This book was developed, designed and produced by David Lane at Legends Publishing. A very big thank you to Keith White at Reduc@te for his support. Other contributors include:

Gayner and Mike Lepic

Nick Norris

Roslyn O'Cionnaith

Jamie Singer

Mark Newton

Tony Kelly

Peter Smith

Mark Adams

Nick Harman

Danielle Haigh-Wood

Alun Thomas

Mads Herholdt

David McCluskey

Jon Page

Ali Maffitt

Caroline Coxon

Grattan Endicot

Simon King

Bill Priddin

Steve Bogg

Stephen Ainscough

Shreya Chakravertty

Mathew Pullen

Keith White

Gary Armstrong

Susan Mowll

David Corcoran

Chris Rigby

Elizabeth Thompson

Deborah Doran

Paul Shinner

To read more stories visit:

WWW.TILIDIE.CO.UK

FURTHER READING

ENGLAND 'TIL I DIE
A celebration of England's amazing supporters

Edited by David Lane

MEYER & MEYER SPORT

This book reveals the funny, the absurd, the emotional, the peculiar, the shocking and unbelievable that is part and parcel of being a die-hard England fan. Tales of unwavering dedication and loyalty, of personal sacrifice and emotional trauma, are entwined with stories highlighting superb camaraderie, intense excitement and proud patriotism. Wives as well as jobs have been lost, overdrafts have plunged to new depths and countless 'sickies' have been thrown—just to be there to cheer on the Three Lions. Real England stories, by real England fans.

My first England game was in 1948, around the same time as the London Olympics, which I also attended. Northern Ireland were the opponents and it was an era when England played against the other home nations far more frequently. There were some cracking players around back then and England were considered pretty invincible, despite slipping up to the occasional defeat to the Auld Enemy. I don't recall having to buy tickets in advance for the terraces and my good friend Terry Kinsley and I used to go regularly. Also, most men worked on Saturday mornings, so there were a lot of fans that went straight to the match from the factories – via the pub of course!

I remember England taking on a Rest of Europe XI in 1953, it was a tremendous match and we drew that game 4-4, but it wasn't the *rest* they needed to fear, it was the *best*, which

GENERATION REX

came in the form of Hungary. I was in awe, as were virtually all of the fans at Wembley that night, all looking on as the Hungarians gave England a footballing lesson. Puskas, Hidegkuti and Kocsis really showed the world, not just the English, what they were capable of. I was standing in line with the penalty area down near the touchline, and I'll never forget watching open-mouthed as Puskas controlled a ball that looked for all the world as if it was going out of play. He backheeled it, then whipped in a wonderful shot from an impossible angle – they toyed with England that evening. As the scoreline stacked up against the home team I don't recall any booing from the crowd, in fact our goalie, Birmingham's Gil Merrick, made some fine saves. From a fan's perspective we simply hadn't seen football played that way before, and I think the English crowd appreciated the good football rather than getting on their side's backs. But worse was to come for England in the return game, when the Hungarians knocked us for seven.

The atmosphere at England matches back then was always good-humoured and lively, but certainly nothing like it is these days with the singing and replica shirt wearing. The noise levels weren't as loud either.

Before moving up to London from Plymouth I always used to listen to England games on the radio, which was always done with a copy of the *Radio Times* close to hand. They always printed a numbered and lettered grid on top of a picture of a tinted football pitch, and as the ball was passed around during the match the commentator would read out the coordinates and you'd move your finger to the appropriate square so that you knew where the ball was. He'd say things

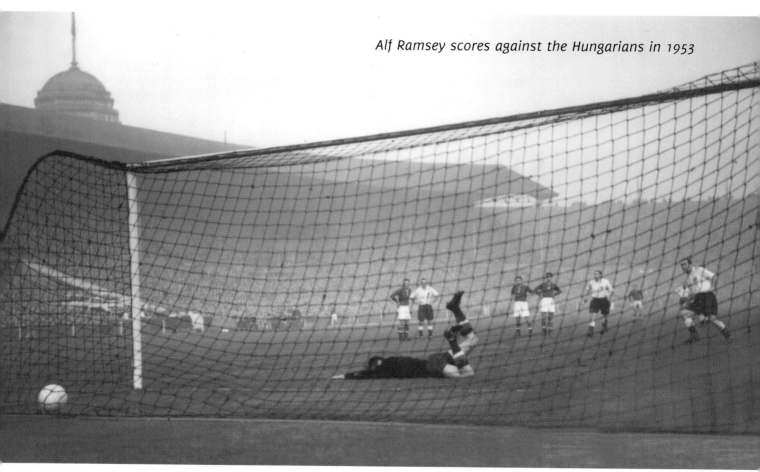

Alf Ramsey scores against the Hungarians in 1953

like: "Now the goalkeeper has the ball, he rolls it out to square 5..." And you'd follow the play like that for the full 90 minutes. It was a little bit different to the coverage on Sky these days!

An infamous game that I also recall listening to on the wireless was England's defeat to the USA at the 1950 World Cup in Brazil. England travelled to the tournament as one of, if not *the*, favourites and, looking through the squad that represented England, there were no lightweights. In my opinion a lot of them were better than some of those who play today. The players are far more athletic and better trained now, granted, but we had some amazing, technically gifted players during that era, players that would hold their own today. Again, I don't recall the players coming home in disgrace or fans waiting at the airport to vent their frustrations as would be the case these days – I think it's only been since the 1970s that the coverage of the England team has reached saturation point and the result of every single match is reported as a life and death fixture, even the friendlies.

I think I'm extremely lucky to have seen some of the greatest ever England players pull on the famous national shirt: players like Billy Wright, Stanley Matthews and Stan Mortensen were special. When I sit at home in the evenings I think back to all the good times, you have to remain positive in life. As you can see from the photo of me on my mobility cart I am extremely proud of being English and supporting our football team. The first thing I did after buying it was to attach a St George's flag to the front and decorate it with England stickers – if I've got to ride around on it I may as well have some fun, that's my outlook. People are always stopping me for a friendly chat, but not everyone has been so pleasant. Believe it or not, I've had a couple of nasty incidents, one from a bloke wearing a Scotland shirt who grabbed me and tried to pull me off the cart, which was very frightening and unnecessary. But I'd never consider removing the flag, why should I? If people have an issue with me driving around flying the flag that's their problem, not mine! I'm proud of being English and proud of my country, so that's the end of it.

Rex Foster

Unfortunately, Rex died since this story was written. It was an honour to have met you, Rex, and Sunbury-upon-Thames misses your spirit.

England 'Til I Die   ISBN 978-1-78255-036-5